The Anglican Church Today:

The Future of Anglicanism

by The Archbishop of Canterbury

Outside the Chapel at Lambeth Palace hang two commemorative tablets. One is an exhortation to remember Archbishop Longley under whose Primacy the first Lambeth Conference was held in 1867. The other is a relief depicting the consecration of Archbishop Matthew Parker 300 years before. It shows the various robes of those who took part–some are in copes, some are wearing gowns, others are in surplices. This diversity of dress signals the mixture of modes of faith and practice behind the Elizabethan Settlement.

This is the enduring legacy of the Anglican Church. Ours is a form of Christianity with a permanent tension between competing opinions. Indeed, it is precisely in living with that tension that our tradition finds its particular genius and its distinctive contribution to the Catholic Church.

But if this claim is to be valid, we must maintain a comprehensiveness that amounts to more than mere coexistence. Today the Anglican Communion is faced with difficulties and controversies which threaten to divide us. If we are to handle such issues with honesty and harmony we need to understand the different strands within Anglicanism, and to cherish the subtle but genuine cohesion that it offers.

These are matters for every Anglican to consider as we make ready for the next Lambeth Conference in 1988. I believe this Series will be of great assistance in this, and I welcome it warmly.

Lambeth Palace, September 1986   + ROBERT CANTUAR

The Anglican Church Today:

The Future of Anglicanism

JOHN WHALE

MOWBRAY

LONDON & OXFORD

First published 1988
by A. R. Mowbray & Co. Ltd,
Saint Thomas House, Becket Street,
Oxford, OX1 1SJ

Typeset by Dataset, Oxford
Printed in Great Britain by Biddles Ltd., Guildford

British Library Cataloguing in Publication Data

Whale, John
The Anglican church today: the future
of Anglicanism. — (Mowbray's Lambeth
series).
1.   Anglican Communion
I.   Title
283   BX5005

ISBN 0–264–67127–9

Contents

1

Diversity

Anglicanism will remain multifarious; and so it should.

It taps multiple sources, in the present as in the past. The three main ones, as countless Anglican apologists have explained, are scripture, tradition and reason. Each of those three has had, and continues to have, its partisans, disposed to value one of them above the other two. Three great interests have grown up within Anglicanism as a result. You can call them by a number of names: low church, high church and broad church; individualism, authority and latitude; Evangelicalism, Catholicism and the middle way.

Each of those tendencies contributes still to the whole. Each has supporters who believe – as how could they not? – that their kind of Anglicanism is the best kind. Some of them, in all three tendencies, go on to the belief that theirs is the one right kind; and they would like to see the whole of the rest of Anglicanism brought over to it, so that Anglicanism the world over became at last one working band, singing one harvest song, and that song their song.

It will not happen. These struggles have been going on since the Reformation. There is no foreseeable likelihood that any of the three tendencies will disappear. Each is too durable, too dearly held, for that.

Fresh signs of these abiding diversities of gifts are to be seen in the three recent books on 'the Anglican Church today' to which this book makes a fourth. The three are *Evangelicals on the Move*, by Michael Saward, a London vicar and a member of the Church of England's General Synod; *Catholics in Crisis*, by Francis Penhale, a sociologist; and *Rediscovering the Middle Way*, by Peter Walker, the Bishop of Ely. I come behind, with the under-informed but uncommitted boldness of the journalist, to peer beyond them at the future. Each of those first three authors allows his readers to perceive how attractive his chosen kind of Anglicanism can be; how loyally it is upheld by its supporters; and how richly it is furnished with attributes that Anglicanism cannot afford to lose.

The Saward book shows Evangelicals to be a body of people who make a confident personal response to a divine revelation. They revere the Bible as disclosing God truly, even if not fully: it is for them the supreme, though not the sole, Christian authority. They set high value on personal conversion, and conversion to a belief in the redeeming work of Christ. They often come to this belief young: Evangelicals are good at camps and movements and missions that engage young people, from children to university students. They subscribe cheerfully to missionary work in other countries besides their own. They take baptism seriously: when the Evangelical clergy baptize babies, they try to ensure a decent measure of commitment in the parents. They also take seriously, when their worship calls for singing, the Psalmist's advice that the song should be a new one: they are constant devisers of new hymns and choruses, with both words and music easy to master. They regularly seek a style of worship that is lively and welcoming. They are persuaded of the usefulness of prayer, and of the divine will and power to answer it. They try, in church and out of it, to use lay as well as clerical leadership. They understand the importance of organization. Their great figures, in the Church of England, have been people like John Newton, the writer of hymns; Charles Simeon, parish minister in Cambridge and organizer of Evangelical patronage; and William Wilberforce and the seventh Lord Shaftesbury, politicians of social reform.

The Penhale book explains Anglican Catholics as people who evoke a partly medieval tradition in order to restore both to religion and to the world surrounding it a sense of the mysterious, the sacred, the enchanted. To that end, they cherish the symbolic, the drama of the sacraments. They cultivate richness in worship: in buildings, ornaments, vestments, music, movement. They respect authority, since it keeps the mystery in expert hands and wards off uncertainty. They see the point of other-worldly spirituality, of monasticism;

they also lay stress on the incarnation as the event through which every activity in this world is touched with the divine. They maintain, as a result, a long-standing readiness for work among their own country's poor. They look back, in the Church of England, to the leaders of the Oxford Movement, especially John Henry Newman, John Keble and Edward Bouverie Pusey; to antiquarians of hymns and liturgy like John Mason Neale; to ritualists like Bishop Edward King of Lincoln; to men of an active political conscience like Stewart Headlam, Bishop Charles Gore of Oxford, and Conrad Noel; and to parish priests like Charles Lowder of London Docks and Alexander Mackonochie of Holborn.

The Walker book celebrates a faithful realism. Followers of the middle way do more than keep an equal distance from the other two tendencies. They perceive that faith changes with the centuries. They acknowledge that modern habits of thought are based on reason rather than on revelation or magic; they know the holes that modern scholarship has made in the fabric of belief. They seek, or approve the search, for new formulations of faith that will accommodate these new realities. They mind about truth. They want Christianity to inhabit the same world as ordinary men and women do. They try in consequence to hold fast to certain central Christian affirmations and sit light to the rest. They make a fundamental belief of the incarnation, but they suspend judgement about how it actually happened. They draw back from dogmas that may exclude certain kinds of believer from their circle of belief. They extend this approach into the search for unity among different Christian denominations, a precious cause to them. The men of this tendency whom the Walker book holds up for special admiration are F. J. A. Hort, the Cambridge New Testament scholar, and Bishop George Bell of Chichester.

It goes without saying that not all believers within the Anglican Communion, which itself extends to ocean's farthest coast, drop into one of these three divisions. There are subdivisions: the Charismatics, notably, within Evangelicalism. Faith is as various as fingerprints are. Many Anglicans belong partly in one group and partly in another. Many find points of sympathy in all three. Yet the classification does cover the main types of Anglican belief. And not just Anglican: constitutional differences aside, most Christian believers of any denomination could discover their counterparts within that range. The three tendencies correspond to abiding and recurrent religious instincts.

A number of consequent observations are in point. First, none of the tendencies can be dismissed as wrong. The claims of each of them are defensible. Within each of them, good and Christian lives have been lived. Upholders of each have shown persuasive signs of knowing God. There clearly are different ways of exploring the unsearchable riches of Christ. The accidents of temperament, of geography, of family influence, of encounters in youth and later life, of words heard and experiences passed through, lead different people in different directions. Whether or not this ought to be so, it is so, and will go on being so, and any forecast of the future of Anglicanism has to take account of it.

Next, therefore, none of the three tendencies is going to disappear. Each will continue to draw a proportion of the available number of believers. The Catholics are in numerical decline at the moment, it seems. But as the old certainties of faith become less and less easy to defend verbally, the stress the Catholics lay on the non-verbal will bring them up again. The Evangelicals are the people of a book, and a book that seems more human and fallible with every volume of biblical studies published. But Evangelicals appear to be growing in numbers, and they represent a longing for textual assurance that is as old and enduring as writing itself. The middle way people are vulnerable to the phenomenon of English politics known as the third-party squeeze, and they are always in the theoretical danger of allowing themselves to be wiped out of existence by the very modesty of their claims. But they are more alert to modern thought than either of the other two groups, they attract more than their share of good minds, and they express the lasting determination in the religious intellect that religion shall not be set apart from other subjects of human enquiry. All three tendencies are likely to survive.

Finally, though, they will never slide into a synthesis. They will certainly not be pushed into it by one tendency's taking the lead over the other two. None can win, or deserves to. It is no more possible to say which of them is right than to say which of a group of contending political parties is right. They are not likely to arrive at synthesis by being guided into it, either. Christians like to talk as if dialogue, assisted perhaps by the Holy Spirit, will one day lead them into truth: that is, into a version of the truth that all can accept. The history, and the current vigour, of religious argument suggests that even the Holy Spirit will find the task discouraging. It is not given to human beings to see truth whole. They see a few of its many faces. Wide differences are likely to persist.

Many Christians find that thought painful. Difference looks like disunity, disloyalty to the faith's founder. They reach for the notion of a core of truth, at any rate, on which everyone can agree. They repeat in various forms the dictum by Peter Meiderlin, of whom nothing is known except that the reluctant dissenter Richard Baxter gives him as its author: 'Unity in things necessary, liberty in things unnecessary, and charity in all.' The sentiment is admirable. The difficulty is in identifying the things necessary. Baxter himself had a different list from the one held by the churchmen who would not stretch their tolerance far enough to keep him and his friends inside the Church of England. Three hundred years on, neither Anglicanism nor the wider Church is any nearer drawing up a common list; and there are few signs that it can be managed at all.

Yet that is not in itself ground for despair. Disunity need not be a prelude to dismemberment and disappearance. It has not so far been. The Christian Church, and Anglicanism as a part of it, is alive and visible across the world. Christian belief is buoyant in developing countries, and durable under Communism; its political and social consequences are endlessly canvassed; a travelling Pope and travelling evangelists pull huge crowds. In the United Kingdom, such statistics as can be had do suggest that churchgoing as a whole is still in decline; but other indices vary the story. Popular interest in the great questions that religion exists to answer – about benign and malign providence, about where human beings fit into the whole pattern of nature, about what happens to them when they die – holds up unabated. Survey evidence continues to suggest that at least a third of the adults in the United Kingdom (a sophisticated society, as societies go) put a religious interpretation on the fragmentary answers that their own experience offers them. The people who run newspapers and broadcasting organizations devote perceptibly more space to serving the religiously interested or curious than they did ten years ago. The audience for religious radio and television holds steady, and may be advancing. Those observations would be even easier to sustain in the United States.

At the same time, much of this widespread religious interest is manifestly outside the Christian Churches. It is expressed by people who know little of denominational dogma and owe no allegiance to it. It is the pressure of the future. As more and more people throughout the world (in absolute if not in proportional terms) are released from an exclusive preoccupation with keeping themselves fed and sheltered, and are able to lift their minds to larger speculations, more and more people will ask questions that are essentially religious. These questioners will appear on the doorsteps of all the Churches. A full share will fall to Anglicanism, with its presence on five continents.

For Anglicanism, the questions will be both a difficulty and an opportunity. On the one hand, to contain its three existing tendencies will be strain enough. No organization would find it easy. Any organization could be forgiven for seeking to stop at that. On the other hand, it is going to be asked to set its bounds wider yet; and it may be doing its proper work if it can consent.

The questioning has begun already. It will touch every part of Anglicanism's life and thought. It will certainly touch doctrine. The three groups so far considered all make the incarnation a centrality. The Anglicanism of the future will be increasingly asked whether it can accept, in addition, believers who look to a merely human Christ. It will be asked to enlarge its understanding of priesthood and episcopacy. It will be asked – this particularly in England – to cut its remaining connections with Government. It will sometimes be asked to become a political force over against Government.

Not all these pressures will it be able to accept. But it has one special aptitude which other great Christian communions do not have in the same measure. It has already learned to contain differing elements. Elizabeth I established the Church of England as a body that spanned the old Romanism and the new Puritanism. There were both Roman Catholics and Puritans who never accepted the settlement, and pulled away from it when they could; but many more dissidents of the same sympathies remained behind, seeking to change the structure from within. With a good deal of bending and creaking, the structure held. Newer provinces of Anglicanism learned in their turn to contain or comprehend divergences. Meanwhile the third force, of reason and historical enquiry, began also to operate. It, too, extended to Anglicanism beyond England. One of its most notorious advocates in the nineteenth century was John William Colenso, a Cornishman who went to South Africa as Bishop of Natal. He proved to be soft on polygamy and unsound on hell. When he was deposed by his metropolitan, Bishop Robert Gray of Cape Town, the Judicial Committee of the Privy Council found in Colenso's favour. Now many Anglicans openly tolerate polygamy (at any rate in Africa) and disbelieve in hell (at any rate in England).

Among people who know little of it, Anglicanism bears a reputation for somnolence. In fact it has been an adventurous Church; and in nothing more adventurous than in matters of doctrine. The theologians who have disturbed the peace of English-speaking Christianity with risky doctrinal speculation in the past hundred and fifty years have in the main been Anglicans. A good proportion of them have been English bishops: Hampden of Hereford, Henson of Hereford and later Durham, Barnes of Birmingham, Robinson of Woolwich, Jenkins of Durham. Storms, demands for excommunication, have descended on their heads; but the storms have passed. Excommunication is not much of an Anglican instrument.

2

Doctrine

More than other denominations, Anglicanism has long lived with doubt. The logical awkwardness of religious certainty has been openly acknowledged by Anglicans for three hundred years at least; and it is too late for that habit of mind to be checked now. Before the end of the seventeenth century, Locke had pointed out – from within the community of Church of England believers – how little grasp we had of God as a matter of knowledge, since knowledge was the outcome of observation and reflection and reason. Revelation produced faith, a different thing; and even then it was a matter for human judgement whether the revelation were divine or not.

It is true that doubt does not seem to have greatly troubled English churchpeople of the eighteenth century. Many of the Church of England clergy in that period spoke and wrote, at least privately, as if the ministry were a way of making a living like any other: easier than many others, since long absences from the place of work, from the parish or diocese, were well within the culture. In that atmosphere, doubt could not be troublesome: the propositions of the faith were to be committed to memory rather than taken to heart. But when earnestness returned, doubt also returned. One of the nineteenth-century poems most admired in its own time, *In Memoriam*, is racked with doubt. Faced with the supreme mysteries of evil and death, all that Tennyson – a loyal son of the rectory – finds himself able to do is 'faintly trust the larger hope'. Again and again (as here in a stanza from section fifty-four, the section Queen Victoria quoted approvingly back to him) he makes Locke's point more gloomily than Locke:

> Behold, we know not anything;
> I can but trust that good shall fall

At last – far off – at last, to all,
And every winter change to spring.

A generation later, in *Robert Elsmere*, Mrs Humphry Ward told the story of a Church of England priest who lost his belief in Jesus's divinity. He left his parish, resigned his orders, and founded a settlement in the East End of London. To his listeners there (in chapter forty) he described the resurrection as an 'exquisite fable'. But he also told them: 'It is your urgent business and mine – at this moment – to do our very *utmost* to bring this life of Jesus, our precious invaluable possession as a people, back into some real and cogent relation with our modern lives and beliefs and hopes.' Published a hundred years ago, in February 1888, the novel was an instant best-seller. My own copy, dated that same year, is from the fourteenth printing.

The twentieth-century Church of England has had recurrent trouble with those two doctrines: both the divinity of Jesus, as certified by his virginal conception, and his bodily resurrection. William Temple, later an Archbishop of Canterbury, was at first refused ordination because he could not confidently accept them. By the time he came, as Archbishop of York, to chair the Doctrine Commission that reported in 1938, he had decided that he could. But he acknowledged that there were scholars and theologians who could not, 'regarding the records rather as parables than as history, a presentation of spiritual truth in narrative form'. Confessed members of that category in recent years have been scholars of the eminence of John Macquarrie, Dennis Nineham and Maurice Wiles.

There are a number of reasons why the Church of England should have been so particularly prone to these questionings. Because the Elizabethan settlement deliberately incorporated more than one Christian tradition into the same whole, and those different traditions remained in varying degrees distinct, it has been easy for the thoughtful worshipper to conclude that there is more than one version of Christian truth. Admit that thought, and you at once have a licence to choose from any version only those parts that you like. It has been one manifestation of the historic problem of Protestantism: the product of fission is itself fissile.

Again, the Church of England has been a body in which the influence of laypeople has been strong. Since the Elizabethan settlement a lay monarch has been its Supreme Governor, and for a couple of centuries was, in fact as well as in name, its bishop-maker. Bishops went on being chosen mainly by the monarch's ministers till 1976. A Parliament largely made up of laypeople sacked several incumbents in the early 1640s and in 1662, and threw out a revised Prayer Book in 1927 and 1928. It was Parliament's redistribution of Irish bishoprics in 1833 that was the proximate cause of the Oxford Movement. The significance of all this is that the Church of England has never been dominated by its clergy. For the clergy, that has had its advantages: they have been spared any serious visitation of anti-clericalism. For the laity, the advantage has been that laypeople too could decently have their own opinions about doctrine. It did not lie wholly under the hand of clerics who might be tempted to keep it complicated.

The Church of England was also the Church which for two or three hundred years a great many people felt obliged to attend, even if they were not Christian believers: certain legal pressures lasted into the nineteenth century, and social pressures well into the twentieth. Indeed, it is probably only since the Second World War in England that the equation between churchgoing and respectability has fallen out of the public mind. Anglicanism in Ireland registers its effects still. The upshot was that there were always a good many natural sceptics in church; and this scepticism was bound to be expressed in private conversation, and sometimes more publicly than that. To this may be added a touch of truculence in the English character, a certain half-articulate reluctance to be told what to think. That characteristic, together with socially enforced churchgoing and the accompanying resentment of it, was also carried abroad to the English colonies that in due time became provinces of the Anglican Communion.

The final, and perhaps the most important, impulse to scepticism within Anglicanism has been the fact of academic freedom. The first Oxford and Cambridge colleges were all clerical foundations. Theology, or a formalized system of

Christian dogmatics, was for centuries the main study there. Even after theology's status as the queen of the sciences had given way to a post-Locke recognition that theological knowledge was in a different category from other kinds of knowledge, theology kept a position of privilege. The regius professors, the canons theologian, stayed in place; and they were all Church of England men. Theology continued to be taught and studied as if it were an academic subject on all fours with philosophy or mathematics. But that meant that in the end it became subject to the same rigorous analysis as philosophy or mathematics. When in the 1850s the Oxford classic and philosopher, Benjamin Jowett, who was also a clergyman of the Church of England, helped put together a discussion by several hands (*Essays and Reviews*) on the Bible, he could not conceal his own finding that the real beliefs of educated people had become separated from Christian teaching, that parts of the Bible which appeared factual were better taken – and still illuminating – as parable or myth, and that miracles and the fulfilment of prophecy were not evidence, as evidence was understood by the modern mind. There was a risk in this kind of writing: some of Jowett's fellow authors were prosecuted from within their own dioceses for heresy, though the prosecutions failed on appeal. But Jowett could not have been true to his surroundings and kept silence: a university exists to pursue truth, and Jowett's central point was that all truth is of God. As other universities were founded in England and all over the Anglican Communion, with a less specifically Christian dedication than Oxford and Cambridge, theologians who worked in them felt all the more of an obligation to behave like academics first and Christian apologists only second. Otherwise the study of theology in those universities might be judged unfitting and expendable. In England lately, in an era of university retrenchment, that has been a lively fear. Although individuals within the Church of England have sometimes responded ungenerously to the exercise of academic freedom, the Church of England corporately has seen the point of it and been in no hurry to inhibit it.

So much for the special reasons for Anglican scepticism. But for the best part of three hundred years it was kept within bounds. A great many Anglicans knew nothing about it at all. It is developments in the past thirty years that have made it important in Anglicanism's future. There are two of them.

One is that this scepticism has come to be much more insistently reported than before. Throughout the West, newspapers and broadcasting have undergone substantial change since the late 1950s. Chiefly it has followed from the establishment of television as a mass medium. News is something that television handles briskly and puts out frequently. In the public at large, the appetite has grown by what it has fed on. The demand for newspapers has increased; or at any rate for grown-up newspapers. (Sales of that British speciality, the popular tabloid, have fallen back a little.) Partly to stimulate and partly to serve that increased demand, newspapers have expanded in size and range. They have been helped by new methods of production. Radio has made a virtue of the ease with which it can be produced and heard, and has expanded too. Television, by making reporters visible, has given all reporters – newspaper and radio reporters as well – a sense that they are entitled to ask their questions because they ask them on behalf of many other people; and the decline in deference has helped them ask awkward questions of people in power.

The world of religion has not escaped this attention. The religiously minded are an interest group to be wooed and served like any other. Reporting of religious affairs is not yet everywhere as advanced as it is in the United States, where many big daily newspapers will run a whole page or more of religious news and comment every Saturday, bordered and economically justified by advertisements for church services to be held next day. That can happen only where the press is arranged regionally more than nationally, and where most readers are therefore within driving distance of the churches advertized. But the scale and penetration of religious reporting in secular organs of opinion in the West in the past thirty years has greatly altered.

Not all of it is well done. Journalists seldom command enough knowledge or enough time for the task in hand. Much newspaper work has to be handed in when the newspaper is ready rather than when the work is ready: it is one of the essential differences between the journalistic and the academic life. Television, the begetter of the changes in question, has not on the whole found (as radio has) that it puts out enough religious news to justify retaining expert reporters. Its specialist reporting effort goes into occasional programmes. In various ways, though, religious news does get increasingly reported.

That has necessarily entailed the reporting of doubt. If a Church's adherents believe what their Church says it believes, that is normal, and journalists are not in the business of reporting the normal: there is too much of it. Doubt, on the other hand, is legitimate news: it is interesting to the public, and sometimes even in the public interest, since word of it can be reassuring or liberating to other people. And the reporting of doubt has concerned Anglicanism more than other denominations, since it is in Anglicanism that doubt has been most prominent.

In England, it was a newspaper article that first publicized Bishop John Robinson's revisionism in *Honest to God*. It was a television series that brought to general view the reductionism of Don Cupitt, a yet more radical Cambridge cleric and theologian. Newspaper reports sold the work of Cupitt, Nineham, Wiles and others in *The Myth of God Incarnate*, a book of essays well enough explained by its title. A television interview, picked up in a popular newspaper, gave notice that there would be frank doctrinal eclecticism from the new Bishop of Durham, David Jenkins.

What was new was not the doubt but the dissemination of doubt. Until this period, news of doubt had been more or less confined to specialist books and journals and church papers. If it penetrated the secular press, it appeared in newspapers that the bulk of the population did not read. Now great numbers of people were exposed both to the fact of doubt within Anglicanism and to the reasons for it, since report was backed with explanation. They began to discover that the evidence for Christianity was not of the kind they had thought it was. You could find weak places in it fairly easily. You could find weak places, and yet remain bound by it, as these theologians clearly did. The system appeared to be sustained as much by itself as by ordinary proof. The evidence for Christianity was in part Christianity itself.

The other considerable change in the public view of religion, in these same past thirty years in the West, has been the increased visibility of other faiths than Christianity. That, too, could not help giving a fillip to Christian doubt. Cults of oriental origin have crossed the Pacific to establish themselves on the western fringes of the United States and Canada, and moved on eastward across the North American continent and thence to Europe. The survival of the young state of Israel, surrounded as it is by its enemies, has reminded the world of the durability of Judaism. Islam, stimulated partly by this hated presence in the Middle East, partly by funds from the huge oil revenues of Islamic countries there, has become notorious for the fervour with which many of its believers uphold its teachings. Immigrant workers into the old industrialized countries have brought their faiths with them and set up their places of worship: England has been made acquainted in this way with Muslims from Pakistan and Sikhs and Hindus from India.

It has become impossible for fair-minded Christians not to perceive that these other sets of beliefs are held by their serious adherents with at least as much assurance as Christianity is. That is bound to touch off in many minds the simple reflection that somebody must be wrong; or, at the very least, that not everybody can be wholly right.

Time was when for Christians that problem could be quickly resolved. If any religion was wrong, it was not Christianity; or not as long as you had hold of the right kind of Christianity. The contention was not frivolous. In the Gifford Lectures he published as *The Philosophy of the Good Life*, Bishop Charles Gore examined non-Christian faiths with unfeigned respect. He nevertheless had little difficulty in concluding that the most satisfactory form of religion was ethical monotheism, and the most satisfactory form of ethical monotheism was Christianity. Somehow that conclusion is not so easy to swallow whole now as it may have been in 1930. In between has come the Second World War, with its disclosure of the bottomless iniquity of which people raised in a Christian tradition are capable; and since then the movement of peoples has meant that many of us have had the beginnings of an education, and needed it, in the force of the Christian maxim – derived from too many of Jesus's stories to be readily set aside – that all human beings are equal in the sight of God. True, we do not have the same authority for believing that all religions are equal in the sight of God. But many Christians have come to suspect that merely to say 'Christianity is best' will not do any more. Some of them have been led to that suspicion by the work of Christian theologians like John Hick and Hans Küng; not Anglicans, as it happens, though they have been joined by Anglicans like John Bowker and Keith Ward. And once you have reached that point you have again begun to concede that there may be respects in which the main Christian claims are not entirely true.

Those two influences – the secular reporting of doubt, and the prominence of non-Christian faiths – must have affected millions of Anglicans worldwide. There is therefore little force left in the argument that to air the fact or the causes of doubt would be to disturb the simple faith of many. It was in the light of that argument that generations of Anglican clergy, having learned of the grounds for doubt at their theological college, went out and never mentioned them in public again. Now, though, simple faith is already widely disturbed. The doctrinal task before churchpeople in the next generation is to offer, to those who want it, a replacement for simple faith. Anglicanism, with its record of theological venturesomeness and elasticity, is equipped for the task, and in certain places is already undertaking it.

Of course it is true that simple faith may still be right. That needs to be regularly said. The Apostles' Creed may be a statement of plain fact from end to end, and we may discover as much with tears of shame and relief when we experience the resurrection of the body ourselves. We certainly cannot prove the Creeds to be false. Miraculous past events are not inconceivable. That all-embracing strain of faith will undoubtedly continue for generations yet, and Anglicans will continue to give it room.

But we can no longer imagine that we can prove the Apostles' Creed to be true, either; or even usefully declare it to be true without qualification. There are too many assertions in it that conflict with the rest of the way we understand our world. The bishops of the Church of England tried a declaratory statement about it in 1986, in a pamphlet called *The Nature of Christian Belief*; and they found themselves obliged to match every declaration with a longer qualification. Qualifications lay particularly thick on 'born of the Virgin Mary' and 'rose again from the dead': the virginal conception and the empty tomb. The pamphlet was a response to protest at the Bishop of Durham's having admitted on television the possibility that neither of those two doctrines was a matter of literal fact. There is a gently sorrowful account of the whole affair in chapter nine of the Bishop of Ely's book on the middle way.

The central issue is divine intervention. That is the religious question which most interests ordinary people, and which Anglicanism will find itself addressing more than any other in the next thirty years. Does God sometimes make things happen that otherwise, in the ordinary chains of human and natural and mechanical causation, would not have happened? Clearly the idea of such activity is coherent. For many people it is covered by a definition: God is a being who behaves like that. But is it a faith that anyone can now claim to live the bulk of a life by? The virginal conception of Jesus and his bodily resurrection, if they happened, happened by divine intervention. That is the point of the doctrines. But if God intervened on those two occasions, why has there been no intervention since? Or if there has, why has it been episodic, stopping one war and allowing another to go on, saving one prayed-for life and letting another be lost? The problem is no less formidable for being familiar.

The fact is that most of us are caught in an inconsistency. We live nearly the whole of our daily lives in the practical belief that things happen because other things cause them to happen. Elijah called down fire from heaven. We strike a match; and if the match will not light we suppose that the box is wet, and if no gas comes out when we turn the gas-tap we conclude that the supply has been cut off because the main is under repair, or that (in the house where I write) we need to install a fresh bottle. Ideas of divine favour or disfavour never enter our heads; or, if they do, we know them to be frivolous. If we took them seriously, we should hardly be able so much as to make ourselves a cup of coffee. Yet under the threat of great evil, of bereavement or war, our minds grope readily for the thought that God might suspend or speed natural forces to help us. Many minds in Britain certainly did during the Falklands war in the summer of 1982; and when British forces recovered the islands after little more than ten weeks of Argentinian occupation, there was a widespread feeling that God had been on the British side, and deserved gratitude for it. Indeed, there was indignation voiced in public, notably by certain Conservative MPs, that the Dean of St Paul's and the Archbishop of Canterbury would not allow the post-war service in St Paul's Cathedral to be a simple shout of thanksgiving, but insisted on the inclusion of such troubling themes as penitence for the failures of foreign policy and grief for the Argentinian as well as the British dead. But it was the MPs who were the more inconsistent. In their workaday identities they believed that success in war required trained forces using efficient equipment. If a British missile had hit an Argentinian warship without exploding, they would have reached for an explanation about a malfunctioning fuse or firing-pin. But when the same thing did indeed happen the other way round, they were ready to believe that God had leaned down to give the British sailors protection. To have said 'God helps those who help themselves' would not have reconciled the contradiction: the maxim amounts to no more than a claim that you succeed if you try hard, which experience in any number of fields – war, politics, running a parish, taking an exam – shows to be plainly untrue.

It is conceivable, certainly, that a divine hand did interfere with the Argentinian fuses. That hypothesis can never be disproved. Christian apologists with a scientific background often point to the irregularities and inexplicabilities in the minutely observed physical universe, and argue that they leave room for the idea of divine action. So they do. The theoretical possibility is not in question. The awkwardness is that not even the most devout Christians conduct their ordinary lives as if the possibility were more than theoretical; and that if it were, the consequent problem of the divine responsibility for evil would make nonsense of the Christian understanding of the divine nature.

It seems to me that an alternative hypothesis is gaining ground, and sure to gain more: the hypothesis of a God who knows all, and loves all, and listens, and suffers with creation; who is therefore still our supreme guide in this life, as the standard by which we set our conduct, and who is also the only hope we have of another life; but who now, in this one, does not act. The agency that does intervene in us is not God but our own idea of God.

That hypothesis will be especially heard within Anglicanism, where reason is admitted as a partner with scripture and tradition. It is already heard. In the summer of 1987 the Church of England's Doctrine Commission – working clerics and academics of various disciplines, not theological tearaways – published a small volume called *We Believe in God*. The final chapter acknowledges that our old ideas about God's control of human affairs will not do any more, and proposes instead two different parallels to explain it. One is with an artist, obliged, however gifted, to work within the constraints of the chosen medium: in this case a human nature endowed with free will. The other is with a parent, yearning after the grown child and yet not able to direct the child's thoughts and actions. Like all parables, these ought not to be pushed too far. But they do indicate that the idea of a non-interventionist God is already within the realm of respectable Anglican discourse.

The members of the Commission contrive to remain stout trinitarians. Not everyone who follows them will be able to do the same. If you accept that there are no divine interventions now, it becomes hard to believe that there were two in fairly rapid succession in Palestine in about 6 BC and AD 30; and still more difficult to accept a third, soon after the second, in the physical arrival of the Holy Spirit. Among English Protestants, to look no wider, there have long been a good many closet unitarians. A human Jesus retains all his power as interpreter of God, teacher of right conduct, and example of the self-forgetful love he preached. Mrs Ward's Robert Elsmere may have been right about that: right, too, in consequence, about the resurrection as an exquisite fable, begotten by 'the devout and passionate fancy of a few mourning Galileans', and yet a fable that was 'a measure of the greatness of Jesus'. And it is perfectly possible to understand the Holy Spirit as a name for our own awareness of God. These are the speculations that will increasingly engage the reasoning Christian mind in any Christian culture which feels that God is not honoured unless truth also is honoured.

Another beautiful and ingenious branch of theology that will come in for consequent reworking is atonement theology. It is already much less preached and written about than it was: people no longer seem sure what to say. The explicitly surviving link with blood sacrifice, the element of bargain, the limitation of benefits to certain categories of people only – all these things are troubling to the modern mind. Yet some doctrine of reconciliation with God is indispensable. Forgiveness is a universal need. In the Lord's Prayer our two primary wants are identified as food and forgiveness. Our observed world is itself forgiving: resentments fade, wounds heal, trees grow again. We cannot believe that a good God is outside this pattern. But we also recognize, in ourselves and in those we know, the truth that we are unfit to be forgiven until we ourselves have been sorry, and have forgiven others whom we have occasion to forgive. If our fallibility is forgivable, so, after all, is other people's. With those observations and others, Anglican theologians will construct altered theories of the way in which the Christian is reconciled to God.

Those theories may or may not include the doctrine of an afterlife. It has always been a doctrine for which there is remarkably little detailed basis in the Bible, and modern research into the paranormal has laid little detail beside that. It is also a doctrine that has not done unmixed good. The idea of a light affliction in this life that wins an eternal weight of glory in another has comforted many in unhappiness. But, like the idea of the divine control of human affairs, it has also dissuaded many from active altruism. If God has everything in hand, and can be relied on to reward the truly deserving either in this world or the next, then human exertion to see that people are properly treated here and now loses its urgency. The question of an afterlife will always be an open one, because neither faith nor reason has much to work on; but even to acknowledge its openness openly will be an advance.

Finally, Christian theologians in the future will be increasingly engaged in accommodating the possibility that non-Christian faiths, too, have hold of part of the truth. Many Christians have been satisfied with quoting Jesus's reported dictum to Thomas, 'No man cometh unto the Father, but by me'. The quotation no longer functions as a proof text. Given the scepticism of many scholars about the authenticity of much of the reported speech in St John's Gospel, it is permissible not to be sure that Jesus said it. If he did say it, he may have been employing his characteristic style of hyperbole: few Christians have regarded 'Take no thought, saying, What shall we eat?' as an instruction to be followed literally. If Jesus said 'No man cometh…' and meant it, he offers an uncharacteristically unattractive picture of a God who sets tests that millions of people have no chance of passing.

It has become much more difficult than it was in the days of Reginald Heber, missionary Bishop of Calcutta, for thoughtful Christians to believe that 'our souls are lighted with wisdom from on high' while everyone else is in darkness. This is easily said, I recognize, from the comparative religious security of the United Kingdom, where Christianity's nominal hold is under no significant proselytizing pressure from any other faith. Things may very well look different to churchpeople in Nigeria, for example, who feel themselves beset by Islam. But the obligation to truth is paramount. If there is a chance that other faiths besides Christianity have access to wisdom from on high, Christians are right to enquire further.

Of the world's 4,800 million people, figures published in 1982 by the *World Christian Encyclopedia* (and quoted in the 1987 English translation of Hans Küng's *Christianity and World Religions*) identify 1,400 million as Christian, 723 million as Muslim, 583 million as Hindu, and 274 million as Buddhist. Judaism is credited with fewer than 20 million;

but its seniority and its political prominence give it an importance beyond its numbers. Those figures mean that although more than a quarter of the world's population is claimed for Christianity, a third of it is claimed for the other world religions. That third represents too large a body of believers to be dismissed. Muslims, most Hindus, and Jews, are fellow monotheists with Christians. In Gautama, Buddhists revere a figure who has many points of similarity with Jesus. There is a weight of religious experience here that deserves to be drawn on.

One consideration in particular makes it likely to be: the threat of war. By the experience of Israel and Northern Ireland, by the struggle between Iran and Iraq, by the recurrent strife on the Indian subcontinent, the world is regularly reminded that religious differences can still lead to pitiless fighting of a kind that could at any time spread. It is a reasonable forecast that, under this stimulus, dialogue between the world religions will be taken up in the 1990s with something of the fervour accorded in the 1960s and 1970s to dialogue between the Christian denominations. The aim of the process, properly enough, will be increased political tolerance. But it would be surprising if there were not also a religious dividend. Christianity, especially, may well learn more from rival faiths than its different denominations ever did from one another: the learning will not be obstructed by the notorious enmity between first cousins. Anglicanism has both the temper and the geographical extent to be among the learners.

3

Antiquity

Churchgoing Christians encounter doctrine in other places besides creeds and sermons. They meet it in all the words they use for worship, and in the pattern of the buildings they worship in. The link remains perceptible. As habits of belief have changed, liturgies and churches have changed. In the Church of England, one communion service, one marriage rite has succeeded another; the towering pulpit of the eighteenth century has given way to the distant chancel of the nineteenth and now the gathered chairs of the twentieth. But there is a natural time-lag, a widespread caution here. Alterations will often be more sharply argued over than alterations in doctrine itself.

Anglicans well understand the power of words and places in which God has long been addressed. As users of words, Anglicans are people of a fixed liturgy: it is one of their principal points of difference from the rest of the Reformed tradition. For many thousands of Sundays, under many different skies, their main service-book was the Book of Common Prayer. In the matter of buildings, the point applies especially to English Anglicans, richly and even heavily endowed still with medieval churches. But it is apt to other Anglicans besides. One of the marks of Anglicanism is to be in communion with the see of Canterbury, and the cathedral there is a place of Anglican pilgrimage from all over the world.

The value of antiquity is continuity. It binds us in a chain of belief. So many other lips have repeated these prayers; so many other feet have worn these stones; and those worshippers seem to have found what they sought in the experience, because they kept returning to it. Following them, we have the sense of not being alone, eccentric. It is human to be reassured by that. More, we sense that in the strength of these words and these walls good lives have been lived; lives of people who have known God. At moments we feel that we might emulate them. However little we succeed, they are part of the testimony that authenticates our faith.

Besides that, continuity is kindly towards believers perplexed by innovation in other things. Precisely at a time when the winds of doctrine are blowing hard, Christians who have no wish to change their beliefs are reminded by the unchanged setting of their worship that they need not: that they remain morally and logically entitled to believe what they were brought up to believe. It may still be entirely true. A traditional setting makes the important point that Anglicanism, whatever else it makes room for, continues to encompass traditional belief.

And continuity speaks of the continuity of God. The four hundred years that a prayer has survived in the same words, the eight hundred years of a church building's life so far: these may be almost invisibly brief periods compared with the eternal changelessness of God, and yet in human terms they are long enough. They are longer than the active life of most comparable human artefacts: other pieces of writing, other buildings. As signs, they serve. They point to the right truth. The things of God last: God lasts. It is the essential ground of faith, and antiquity in buildings and worship nourishes it.

All that has weight. Yet there is also a decent case for change in these things. Buildings decay and fall, their maintenance becomes crushingly expensive, they no longer make physical allowance for the things congregations want to do, they turn out to be in the wrong places or not to be in the right ones. Words lose their immediate intelligibility, they change their sense, they take on a strangeness that separates religion from common life, they express attitudes of mind (towards women, for example) that many people no longer hold, they emphasize past belief at the expense of present belief. Both buildings and words need to show that the present-day architect and the present-day writer are as active in the service of God as their predecessors were. Otherwise, religion is misrepresented as a dying influence. Worship needs modernity as well as antiquity.

As so often, right judgement is a question of balance. Within the Anglican Communion, the chief custodian of old words and old stones is necessarily the Church of England; and not in the end the Church of England corporately, but thousands of individual incumbents and church councils. My guess, a little gloomily made, is that these people will go on inclining the balance against old words and in favour of old stones.

The Church of England has never had much of a taste for extempore speech in church. When it is well done it can achieve directness and warmth; but Church of England congregations are quick, perhaps too quick, to be embarrassed, and they prefer the safety of pre-ordained forms of words, even at the price of a little coolness. In general, though, leaders in the Church of England have recognized that congregations differ, and that it is shrewd to let more than one form be pre-ordained. One among the Thirty-nine Articles that would still command wide assent, the thirty-fourth, says in terms: 'It is not necessary that traditions and ceremonies be in all places one, or utterly like, for at all times thay have been diverse, and may be changed according to the diversity of countries, times, and men's manners, so that nothing be ordained against God's word' (*so that* in the sense of *provided that*).

For a while this wise line was not held. As an outcome of the religious struggles of the seventeenth century, the Book of Common Prayer was protected with all the rigour of the law. Incumbents were to use it and nothing else. After the legal discouragements to Nonconformist and Roman Catholic worship had been lifted in the early part of the nineteenth century, liturgical diversity gradually established itself within, as well as outside, the Church of England; and by the beginning of the twentieth the level of anarchy was such that, after a royal commission had reported, a new Prayer Book was put in hand in an attempt to let the law catch up with custom. Although it failed in Parliament, the new book was the beginning of the laborious process of liturgical discussion and experiment, gathering speed in the 1960s, which finally resulted in the Alternative Service Book of 1980. Itself a variant to the Book of Common Prayer, it contained several variant versions of its own services. The principle of controlled diversity was restored.

The sequence of events was understandable enough, but it was unlucky in the date when it ended. Perhaps no date would have been a good date. Certainly 1980 was an unfortunate one. The 1960s and 1970s were not a period when English prose was well understood. The people who put the Alternative Service Book together had little perception of the qualities that had helped Cranmer and his successors when they compiled the Book of Common Prayer: the ear for the music of varied vowel sounds, the affection for antithesis, the feeling for a sentence's shape and cadence, the knack of setting off plain words with an occasional less plain one ('that we may be defended from all *adversities* which may happen to the body, and from all evil thoughts which may assault and hurt the soul'). These are devices of rhetoric, and rhetoric was especially distrusted in England in so unauthoritarian an age as the 1960s and 1970s.

More than that, though, it was just the age when doubt within the Church of England was beginning to become public. The prayers in the Alternative Service Book claimed a degree of doctrinal assurance that was no longer there. The compilers had little other option: new assurances were not yet in place. Perhaps they never will be. Perhaps it will never be possible to make a good prayer-book again. To write good prose you need to be sure of what you think; English liturgists may never recover that condition of mind.

The compilers might have done better to do as the Church in Wales has done, and confine themselves to revising the Book of Common Prayer, making only such changes as modern usage required. The effect in the Welsh book is a little antiquarian: the new phrases draw too much attention to the oldness of the old. But there are certain advantages. The broad familiarity of the words does mean that the middle-aged and elderly who come to church only occasionally (for rites of passage, for example) are not discomforted by the sense of recognizing nothing. And antiquarianism has its doctrinal convenience. Although many petitions in the Book of Common

Prayer ask for divine action only in us, many ask for it in the external world: 'that it may please thee to preserve all that travel by land or by water...' Disbelievers in that kind of divine action can still assent to the prayer in good conscience, mentally rewriting it as a reminder that when we travel we should be especially aware of God and our inevitable end, and drive carefully ourselves as agents of the divine concern; and they can accept the phraseology as an expression of the way people thought when the prayer was written. That is less easy if the same kind of sentiment appears in modern language.

In spite of all that, the Alternative Service Book does seem to have been widely and cheerfully accepted in the first seven years after its publication. In the same way, new translations of the Bible have made head against the Authorized Version and Coverdale's translation of the Psalms (both Anglican in origin, though neither exclusively so in use). Coverdale, the Book of Common Prayer and the Authorized Version can still be found in regular use in English churches by the worshipper who looks for them, but the search is easier in well-churched cities than in the suburbs or the country.

The present Archbishop of York, John Habgood, himself one of the Alternative Service Book's begetters, suggested in 1983 (in chapter eight of his book *Church and Nation in a Secular Age*) that groups of churches should band together to see that in each area there was a proper choice of old forms of service and new, with some churches offering only one and some only the other, so that local people knew what to expect where. It is a good idea; and there would be a case for matching words to buildings, so that in a certain number of pre-nineteenth-century churches the liturgy and the architecture supported one another in their witness to the continuity of belief. The old cathedrals would serve this cause particularly well. But I know of no evidence that anything of this kind happens. Church councils and cathedral chapters value their autonomy in matters of worship, and keep it exercised.

On the whole, the new gains on the old. The virtues of modernity are valued above the virtues of antiquity. That balance is not likely to change. The most that is likely to happen is that, in the next decade or so, the General Synod of the Church of England will continue to authorize services that meet needs not recognized when the Alternative Service Book was published. These might be services of prayer and dedication after civil marriage, or eucharistic prayers to be used with children; and perhaps also versions of the most popular services – communion, evensong, marriage, burial – compiled from the phrases of the Book of Common Prayer. Some of these latter exist already, mostly derived from the original by way of the 1928 book. A communion service of that kind can be teased out of the second communion rite in the Alternative Service Book itself, if you take the right options. At the turn of the century those extra services might well find themselves gathered into a new supplement to the Alternative Service Book; and in due time a new edition of the book might class them among the wheat rather than the tares. It is hard to offer Prayer Book loyalists any livelier hope than that.

The problem of old buildings is different. It is not a problem of impending disappearance. Indeed, the Church of England's chief difficulty about old churches is that it has too many of them. There has always been over-supply: a church for every parish, in town and country, and many parishes very small. In medieval Norwich or York, there was a church for every four hundred souls at most – men, women and children. When Canaletto was in London in the 1750s and set up his easel on the empty rising ground north of Clerkenwell to look down towards St Paul's, he could see thirty-five spires within a mile or so of the cathedral. The subsequent movement of the citizens westward made the excess even more marked. And in the nineteenth century, idealists built big churches for the spreading suburbs and the new industrial towns in the faith rather than the knowledge that they would be useful.

By the end of the twentieth century, the mere passage of time has set a high value on the whole of this huge inheritance, and the Church of England's adherents and friends, little helped from public funds, have to keep it in shape. The old cathedrals survive well enough: they appeal regularly for large sums of money, and usually get what they ask for. But country churches live much more tenuously than that. In England there are nine thousand villages that have a population of less than five hundred, and most of them have an old church. (The statistic is from a 1986 report to the General Synod by the Bishop of Norwich and Anthony Russell called *A Rural Strategy for the Church of England*.) For many travellers, country churches are part of the Englishness of England, and widespread distress would follow any demolition. Yet the burden of maintenance on those handfuls of people, not all of them well disposed to the Church of England, can be heavy. As for town and suburban churches, mostly built or enlarged in the nineteenth century, it is a quirk of misfortune for the Church of England that in the past thirty years, while the congregations of those churches have for the most part diminished, their architecture has become fashionable. The temptation to knock them down and make money on the site is not one that the Church of England can at present yield to and avoid a charge of vandalism.

The Church of England has its machinery for disposing of unwanted churches, and some dozens of them have been made over to the limited range of semi-secular uses judged generally acceptable. Organ-building and wood-carving go forward. A church in Oxford has become a college library. Of two well known examples in central London, one has become a religious publishing house and the other a concert hall.

It is a reasonable prediction that economic pressures will widen that range. There has been little problem about letting these churches go as places of worship to other Christian denominations, whatever the sense of failure entailed. Denominations mainly serving black worshippers have been regular customers, especially in the inner suburbs of big cities. There has been more difficulty about selling churches to other faiths. The sale of an unwanted nineteenth-century church in Southampton in 1983 to a *gurdwara* or congregation of Sikhs was strongly opposed in the General Synod before it was finally approved by the Church Commissioners. The ground of opposition was that such a sale would make the Church of England appear to think one religion as true as another. Without ever thinking that, the Church of England is likely to move nearer the belief that no religion has a monopoly of truth, and the transfer of churches to other religions will be eased as a result.

Straightforwardly secular uses may be expected to increase, too: of churches as private houses, and blocks of flats, and printing-works, and small factories, and do-it-yourself stores, and garden centres. Those last two are after all two magnets that attract English families on Sundays, and the pursuits they foster are innocent and familial enough. A precondition is that the restrictions on Sunday trading in England and Wales should be tidied in the one way that will be found to make sense, which is to remove them all. When the attempt was made in 1985 and 1986, the Church of England was among the bodies that resisted it.

And there will be more demolition. It is impossible to believe that the fashion for nineteenth-century architects will persist at its present intensity. It is fair that they should have been rescued from the facile scorn visited on them in the second quarter of the twentieth century. But there is no blinking the fact that the architecture of most churches built in the latter half of the nineteenth century, in England and in places of English influence abroad, is derivative. It followed its medieval Gothic models for high liturgical reasons, and it went beyond them, particularly in its use of colour. Yet even the best work of William Butterfield or George Edmund Street or Alfred Waterhouse or Sir George Gilbert Scott is in the end more of a copy than an original. It has something of the quality of Milton's Latin verse: remarkable as it is for taste and skill, it has little to do with the age it came from, and you wonder why so much intellectual energy was not deployed on fresher work.

Some of the demolition will be partial. In the preservationist 1980s, architects have become skilful at working round preservation orders by incorporating parts of old buildings into new. The surviving part serves as a decent memorial to the old whole. The technique can work as well with churches as with secular buildings, and can be applied to conjunctions that bring churches into contact with secular buildings. Churches neither need nor ought to be invariably insulated from the secular world.

All these things will happen. But they will not happen enough. A disproportionate share of churchpeople's time will still be taken up with the maintenance of old buildings in something near their old state. They are a more visible and intelligible obligation than old words. The activity is not harmful in itself: many congregations have found that raising money for the roof fund has given them a fellowship they lacked before. But there are many other good causes to raise money for, many other good objects to spend time on. The concern for old buildings can shift out of balance.

4

Priesthood

Equipped with doctrines, services and buildings, a Church still needs ministers. The term 'priest' is not to everyone's liking, but I use it as a technical term, meaning someone authorized to perform all ceremonies except those few reserved for bishops. It is in its priesthood that Anglicanism is undergoing the most noticeable changes of all. The Anglican ministry is now admitting part-timers, the divorced, and women. The scale of these innovations will increase. There are respectable arguments against all of them, but in the end the logic of them will not be denied.

Unpaid, part-time clergy – non-stipendiary ministers, in England – have become familiar figures in many parishes in the past couple of decades. During the day they do the secular work that earns them a living: a lot of them are teachers, though the total spread of trades represented is wide. At evenings and weekends they are available as clergy; and some of them for longer than that, being already pensioned. The reasons for the new pattern are clear enough. Over the centuries the clergy have moved from being the only educated people in society to being one educated group among many. Even theologically, laypeople are better educated than they were. They also live longer than they did, and yet sometimes retire earlier, so that in the latter third or so of their active lives they can represent an under-used supply of intellectual energy.

At the same time, the stock of paid, full-time priests has suffered a falling off. It is sufficiently explained by falling numbers of steady worshippers, who are both the source and the main economic support of a full-time ministry. This falling off has been particularly marked in the English countryside.

The old ideal of a priest in each parish has always been patchily upheld; but in the past generation it has broken down altogether, and groups of as many as ten villages have been gathered into the care of ministers working as a team or even by themselves. Team arrangements do at any rate relieve the loneliness of the clerical life, and they deliver a parish from falling into the hands of a single unchanging incompetent; but they are not liked. Most parishioners would much rather have their own ministers again.

So a supply encounters a demand. The use made of the supply will undoubtedly grow. More and more part-timers will be recruited, and more and more of them will have charge of parishes of their own. Sometimes their orders will be valid in the first instance only within their own parishes. Experiments on those lines have already begun. A part-time ministry is not beyond reproach; but the reproaches can be answered. The formal ministerial training of part-timers, being largely acquired in the evenings and at weekends, is less thorough than full-timers had at their theological colleges; but it may be fresher. Part-timers are not always on hand to meet pastoral needs or administer rites of passage; but even intermittent local provision may be better than no local provision at all. Not being economically dependent on the work, part-timers are less completely at a bishop's or an archdeacon's orders than full-timers, and may sometimes default on obligations they have taken up; but the problem can be lessened by a system of contracts for fixed terms. Part-timers may sometimes be seen as short on personal holiness; but there are other kinds of holiness besides removal from the secular world, and in the person of part-timers the Church is able to penetrate the secular world at the place of work, though the usefulness of that ought not to be over-emphasized. Part-time ministry will increase, and churchpeople will learn to extract the good from it as best they can.

The Church and the world do interpenetrate, whether the Church likes it or not. One of the areas where the Church cannot avoid the influence of the world is marriage. Monogamy is both a good thing for the couple concerned, as certified still by the experience of millions, and convenient for society at large as providing the least unsatisfactory framework for the bringing up of the next generation. Because some (though not all) of Jesus's reported sayings about marriage support a high view of it, and because many couples wish to make their promises to one another in the sight and the house of God, and because the clergy preach over them there, it is to the clergy that society on the whole devolves the function of speaking in monogamy's praise. It is therefore embarrassing to both society and clergy when the clergy fail to uphold monogamy in their own lives. The rate at which clergy marriages break up, or at which the clergy take spouses who have themselves been divorced, is probably less than for other groups of people. The clergy would try particularly hard to avoid giving that kind of offence. Nevertheless, the contagion of the world's slow stain is not to be avoided altogether. The phenomenon of the divorced priest, or of the priest married to a divorced partner, is increasing within Anglicanism, and is bound to increase further. No rules to restrain it could be fair in individual cases. Differences between different Anglican provinces will reflect only the custom of the country. It is a melancholy forecast, but an inescapable one. Bishops and church councils will retain their present discretion, but will exercise it indulgently while society is indulgent. They will be right. Forgiveness is in the end more Christian than condemnation.

To the world at large, by far the most interesting present change in the Anglican priesthood is the slow change to women priests. They are already licensed in about a quarter of the provinces of the Anglican Communion; it is a safe prediction that they will come in the rest. The only remaining uncertainty is the date.

In all of Anglicanism the sternest objections, sterner even than from Australia, have been heard from within the Church of England; and the struggle against women priests was for practical purposes lost in the Church of England by the series of votes in its General Synod on the measure allowing women to be ordained as deacons. Once safely approved by Parliament and the Crown, it took effect in February 1987, and the ordinations began the same month. Advocates of the priesthood of women were careful not to crow, but they knew the advantage they now held.

The measure had originally been put forward as a mere piece of clarification: women had been deaconesses since the middle of the nineteenth century, but it was not clear whether in that status they were in holy orders or not, and they deserved to know where they stood. If they became deacons, they would still be a safe distance from attaining the power to celebrate communion, which had become the point of contention on both sides. Opponents of women priests were divided. A number of them believed that here was a harmless concession which would buy the advocates off. Generously made, it could expect a generous response.

The fact was that in not contesting this particular skirmish the opponents were conceding the war. The distinction they were left defending looked absurdly narrow. As deacons, women could suddenly take marriage services; they could wear clerical collars; they could be called 'the Reverend'. (Within five months the first of them was entitled to be called 'the Reverend Canon', in the diocese of Worcester, where canons need only be clerks in holy orders, not priests.) To the secular world, the world that encountered the clergy at weddings and in the pages of the local newspaper, this was precisely what being a priest consisted in. Women had achieved it. The argument was ended. The attempt to renew it over a single service would be met with widespread incomprehension.

In the struggle for the good opinion of churchpeople, too, the measure allowed women to make an important advance. The first groups of women who came forward in each diocese to be deaconed were an impressive lot. It was natural that they should be. They represented the accumulation of several years of waiting: they were in the main experienced, thoughtful and resolute. Dispatched often to parishes where they had not served before, they would release new energies in themselves and others. They would be walking evidence that the ministry of women worked, and they had a strong chance of winning over even its opponents. Opinion would be progressively softened in their favour.

The stately processes of the Synod mean that there can be no women priests proper in the Church of England until the 1990s. However irritating this slow pace may have been to English advocates of the priesting of women, it has in fact prospered their cause. By the time the change is formally made, the heat will have gone out of it. Whether cheerfully or resignedly, most churchpeople will have become used to the idea. The secessions that have beset the Episcopal Church in the United States will be on a far smaller scale in the Church of England; and even at that they will seem disproportionate. Women will be able to begin their priestly ministry in England in an atmosphere of calm.

It will have been one of those rare religious arguments where scripture and tradition have been overborne by reason. The arguments from scripture are tolerably clear, and they do little for women priests. Jesus appears to have had no women disciples, though he did have women friends; and St Paul, rule-making for the first Christians, thought women should be submissive and silent. You can say there was no developed priesthood then: it is still clear that, in whatever religious organization either Jesus or Paul knew, women had no prominent part. You can say that all this was only the outcome of the age they lived in, and should carry no message for later times and cultures. If you believe in the incarnation, though, as a divine intervention, then the Middle East in the first century AD was the place and time God chose, and the rest of us have to live with that.

The arguments from tradition are similarly unencouraging to women priests. For nineteen centuries the whole Christian Church did without them. Furthermore, during that time there developed the doctrine that it was the business of the priest to represent Christ, and even God, to the congregation. Christ was indubitably male, and it occurred to no one to doubt that God was too. You could only dispute whether such a tradition ought to have grown up; not whether it had.

The argument that is wearing those down is an argument purely from reason, and secular reason at that. It points out that in the West the Christian priesthood is now the last profession left where there is substantial opposition to the entry of women, and that there is nothing about the priesthood which justifies this separate status. Long familiar with women writers and artists, in the latter half of the twentieth century the developed world has become used to women cabinet ministers, women judges, women officers in the forces, women editors, women publishers, women managers in business and industry, women civil servants, women local-government officials, women academics, women scientists, and so on. Nearly all those lines of work were at one time considered naturally closed to women. Now, in the light of experience, no one can plausibly claim that women as a class are less well endowed for them than men. The case is that the Christian priesthood is an exactly parallel line of work, calling on similar qualities of judgement and articulacy. Further, even those jobs from which women used to be kept by their comparative physical weakness, like bus-driving or printing, have been opened to them as the equipment has become lighter to operate. In the same way the risks and fatigues of a priest's pastoral visiting, for example, have been much reduced by the invention of the motor-car and the telephone. Conversely, men have now moved into work that used to be considered the preserve of women, like nursing. In general, work is no longer distributed by gender; and where it is, it ought not to be, since such a distribution is both wasteful and unfair.

Christians are awkwardly placed for denying that drift of argument. They thought of it first, and they wish to use it still in other contexts. Much of the impetus behind the emancipation of women in this century, as also behind the establishment of a manhood suffrage before that, came from ideas about the equal weight of all human beings in the only judgement that mattered, which was God's. Those ideas were directly derived from the recorded sayings and stories of Jesus. The same ideas are still being actively deployed by Christians, and still on behalf of women. A newspaper inset published in November 1986 by the Anglican Consultative Council, for example, and entitled *Peace and Justice: a Working Paper for Lambeth 1988*, contends: 'The oppression of women is certainly the oldest form of oppression in human history ... Women have always known who weeds the sorghum, transplants the rice seedlings, picks the beans, tends the chickens. In Africa, for instance, women do three-quarters of the argricultural work and grow ninety per cent of the food for family consumption, yet they are not recognized as farmers. All the aid and technical advice goes to men ... The present world economic order exploits Asian women as cheap labour in agriculture and industry and exports them for the same purpose as migrant workers and mail-order brides ... Brutal husbands can be found at all levels of society ... The Church has a particular responsibility for vigilance in human-rights matters ...'

It can be legitimately objected that access to the priesthood is not a human right in the same sense that fair reward for work or protection from attack are human rights. Priests, after all, need a certain specialist education, and there is nothing unjust about turning down applicants who are without it. Nevertheless, it is in practice virtually impossible for Christians to go on demanding the emancipation of women in the name of Christ and at the same time leaving them widely unemancipated within certain Christian organizations. The secular world is simply not going to perceive the justifying nuance.

The dispute has already caused disproportionate distress within the Anglican Communion. It is important that its ending should add as little to that unhappiness as possible. The clinching arguments will need choosing with care. In chapter nine of his book on Anglican Catholics, Francis Penhale suggests that in the opposition to women priests from men priests there may be a trace of homosexual misogyny. It is useful to have the question openly raised; and once it is recognized that homosexuals are as much part of God's creation as anyone else (another proper Christian cause), their views can form part of the public discussion. Till then, Anglicans will be well advised to hold to the high ground. Motives may be equally complicated on the other side, after all: among certain women by worldly ambition, for example.

The arguing stage is nearly over. The next concern will be to see that the introduction of women priests into those Anglican provinces that do not already ordain them is as little painful as possible to continuing objectors. The essential principle will again be controlled diversity. Just as the 1978 Lambeth Conference formally declared its acceptance both of those provinces that ordained women and of those that did not, so provinces moving a decade later from the second category to the first will wish to make sure that parishes and priests and bishops unable to countenance the priesthood of women will have at any rate the temporary liberty of declining it. In the Church of England, bishops already have the right to refuse to ordain, institute or license; incumbents are entitled to reject the services of any priestly colleague offered them; parishes with a resolute church council have the *de facto* power to turn down an unwanted incumbent. These powers will need to be codified in a new measure; otherwise their use will fall foul of secular legislation (the Sex Discrimination Act 1975). The measure could have a limited life of, say, ten years. During that time a number of the objecting bishops, priests and parish activists would retire or die; and their replacements would in the nature of things be mainly people who had perceived the direction of events and accepted it. If that had not happened, the life of the measure could be prolonged piecemeal until it had.

The essential is time. A course set over centuries may well need decades to alter. In the United States, it seems to have been the comparative suddenness of the move to women priests that occasioned the subsequent divisions. The point is worth pausing on, because American zeal for total change as soon as the case for change is made out may now induce the same difficulties in the Anglican Communion as a whole. The issue this time will be women bishops. Long before the 1988 Lambeth Conference, it was certain to be the topic that interested the secular press most.

On the one hand, there is no essential sacramental distinction between the office of priest and the office of bishop. The English bishops have said as much (in a 1987 report to the General Synod, *The Ordination of Women to the Priesthood*). If women can fill one, they can fill the other. Men become potential candidates for the episcopate some ten or fifteen years after their ordination as priest; the Episcopal Church in the United States now has a number of women in that category, and some have already been put forward as candidates, though without being chosen. On the other hand, most of the other provinces of the Anglican Communion have not even reached the stage of ordaining women as priests yet. If the Americans go ahead and make a woman bishop, some of those other provinces may feel that their consent is being presumed on; that in so visible a matter as this, the Anglican Communion ought to move more or less as one; and that if it does not, it has ceased to have much reality as a corporate body. On the worst hypothesis, provinces of that persuasion will withdraw from the Communion altogether.

It would clearly be convenient if the three East-Coast American diocesans reportedly resolved to wait no longer than the end of the 1988 Lambeth Conference before they set about securing a woman assistant could wait a little longer yet. No overriding principle would be flouted: to become a bishop is even less of a universal human right than to become a priest. If the Americans could wait, at a minimum, till all the other Anglican provinces had cancelled their objection to the ordination of women as priests, the Anglican Communion would not then be doing diametrically different things in different parts. The dilemma is an intriguing test of the strength of the Anglican Communion as an idea; and yet a stiff test, since the competing idea is one of the most powerful of the twentieth century. If the Americans are prepared to wait, they will be upholding Anglicanism; if they press ahead, they will be preferring feminism.

It is a sound journalistic maxim, current on good newspapers to quell the alarmism that makes for strong opening paragraphs, that the worst seldom happens. In sub-editors' parlance, rows loom more often than they erupt. Within the Church of England, there has already been a cooling off in the talk about parishes that would reject the authority of any bishop who priested a woman, and about other bishops who would lead them off in a secession. As the point of uncomfortable decision comes nearer, the talk will cool further. Another prediction can be safely made. A schism on this issue will never prosper. The emancipation of women is not a fashion, due to disappear in the next generation: it is an idea whose justice and wisdom has been recognized, once for all. Any Anglicans who went into schism as a protest against a female priesthood or episcopate could never carry enough popular support with them to survive. They would claim, as schismatics regularly do, that it was not they who were leaving the main body so much as the main body which was leaving them; but they would not be believed. The need for the main body to develop as it had would be well enough understood.

There will doubtless be a few schismatics. After a while they will fade away like the Nonjurors, upright men who at the end of the seventeenth century left their bishoprics and parishes rather than swear allegiance to William and Mary. They mistook the tradition of a hereditary monarchy for a principle. The tradition of an all-male priesthood will come to seem as impermanent. And in a hundred years' time, students of late-twentieth-century church history will rub their eyes over the fuss with as much astonishment as we now do over the late-nineteenth-century squabbles about candles on the altar.

5

Episcopacy

There are more interesting questions about bishops than whether some of them will one day be women.

Bishops are one of the distinguishing signs of Anglicanism, and identified as such. They are the fourth of the four sides of the Lambeth Quadrilateral, that definition of Anglican essentials adapted by the 1888 Lambeth Conference from an Episcopalian gathering in Chicago two years before. (The first three are the Bible, the Creeds and the Gospel sacraments.) Bishops mark Anglicanism off from most of the rest of the Reformed tradition. They are Anglicanism's claim to have a structure of authority that all other Churches would recognize.

But at once we encounter a practical difficulty. Bishops are strikingly short of authority. Anglicanism is now synodical; and bishops make up merely part of a synod, and are regularly voted down by the whole. It happens in the General Synod of the Church of England. In 1972, for example, the Synod's House of Bishops voted heavily in favour of the scheme for reunion between Anglicans and Methodists; but the Houses of Clergy and Laity gave it inadequate majorities, and it fell. Ten years later a similar fate overtook the proposed covenant under which the Church of England would recognize the validity of ordination in various Free Churches (Methodist, United Reformed, Moravian), and those Churches would accept episcopal oversight. In 1985 the bishops abandoned their long search for a way of approving the remarriage of certain divorced people in church: the obstacle was opposition in diocesan synods.

Synods are not ideal instruments of church leadership. Like the conferences of trade unions and political parties, they can represent the activist more accurately than the ordinary supporter. Their numbers are so large and shifting that it is difficult for them to pursue a steady line. But both where the Church of England's General Synod has been adventurous, as in liturgical reform, and where it has been cautious, as in most questions of church order, it seems to have come tolerably near the temper of ordinary churchgoers. The system suits the times. A United Kingdom Parliament with only a handful of Church of England churchgoers in it is no longer equipped for detailed scrutiny of the Church of England's affairs; and in these argumentative days neither laity nor clergy would be happy to leave everything in the hands of the bishops. Synods are non-autocratic, and in that they have the future of Anglicanism with them.

And bishops are not useless for having shed some of their authority to assemblies that wield it a little clumsily. Although bishops no longer command, they represent. A world that has taken away one of their functions has conferred on them a new one. Modern journalism makes bishops important as representatives. Trading in the questions of the hour, printed and broadcast journalism needs opinions. Sometimes it needs them from Churches, and Churches sometimes have opinions they would like published. To present opinions, journalism needs people: at best, people whom its readers and listeners and viewers have heard of, and are interested to have opinions from. Here comes in the advantage of a settled leadership, as distinct from the revolving style favoured for good egalitarian reasons by the Free Churches. The bishop, the archbishop, is known; worth talking to; worth listening to.

Consulted in this way, bishops speak to a good many of the clergy and laity they serve. But they also speak for them. Indeed, the effectiveness with which they exercise this new kind of authority will depend on their accuracy as representatives. The opportunities themselves are fragmentary, and presented on journalists' capricious terms. Patiently and gracefully used, though, they amount to an extension of Christian influence in a world where such things have become rare.

There is nevertheless a corollary to that. It is that the number of bishops ought not to go on increasing. In England, by the middle of the nineteenth century, changes in population had certainly made the bishops look insufficient and ill-distributed, especially in the North; and the new dioceses founded in the fifty years from 1877, and the institution of suffragans at the same time, were necessary enough. But it is noticeable that since then the number of suffragans has gone on rising even while the number of churchgoers has been falling; and the pressure for more, and for more dioceses, is not spent yet. The office of bishop has a touch of mystery, not to say make-believe, about it. The rest of us are asked to believe – wish to believe – that here is someone peculiarly endowed with wisdom and grace. The magic is easier to sustain if we are not asked to believe that too often. The influence of bishops, with their own charges as much as with journalists, depends to some extent on their rarity.

That creates a difficulty, admittedly. Diocesan bishops are among the most hard-worked people in England. Besides being representatives, they are managers, particularly of their clergy. The clergy can absorb any amount of managing: they are sensitive people, working mostly alone, for inadequate material reward and often with little sense of professional success. Faced with the task of encouraging these people, and conscious of where their own duty is owed, bishops are never likely to consider their work done. It is the kind of work which expands irresistibly to fill the time available. Even doubling the existing number of bishops would hardly help: the new ones would face the same expansion, and their charges would feel that the supply of wisdom had been diluted.

To lessen the problem, bishops will more and more be chosen as managers, so that they can make the most of the time they have. The day of the former headmaster, even the former professor of theology, is done. They will be chosen for their good sense in seeing what tasks are worth attempting, for their judgement in deciding how the people available are best disposed, for their firmness in bringing that disposition about, for their openness in telling as many people as possible what is being done, for their deftness in dispatching all the paperwork entailed. The wisdom to be representatives they will have to find on top of all that.

This has two consequences. First, they will not be chosen for their churchmanship; or at any rate it will be low on the list of criteria. In the third chapter of his book about Evangelicals, Michael Saward rightly points out that in England the Evangelicals have long been hard done by in the matter of bishoprics, to say nothing of lesser dignities. In so far as this follows from a preference among the choosers of bishops for candidates from the Catholic wing or the middle ground, I think it is likely to come to an end. But that is not to say that there will be a great many more Evangelical bishops, either. It is part of efficient management (as it is of Christian behaviour in general) to perceive the good in everyone. Nothing of value should be wasted. The quality that will be looked for in future bishops is a wide tolerance in the matter of churchmanship, a readiness to respect and preserve and use whatever kind is offered, in people or parishes. Bishops commonly lose the angularity of their churchmanship once they become bishops. The same thing will happen more and more to potential bishops.

Second, bishops will not be loved. They are in any case likely to be without the loyalty accorded on grounds of churchmanship. More than that, though, the qualities that make good managers are not lovable. Managers may themselves love their charges, but they must not expect to be loved by them. You cannot oblige people to do what they are reluctant to do, or to stop doing what they enjoy doing, or to lay aside a plan dear to them, or to swallow certain awkward truths about themselves, and expect to retain their active affection. Perhaps bishops never have been as well loved as the memorial tablets claim. It is noticeable that beloved bishops, like miracles, are always in the past. Either way, their chances of being beloved in the future dwindle.

That in turn complicates another question, which is the matter of election. Everywhere else in the Anglican Communion except in England, bishops are elected. That alone makes it probable that before very long they will be elected in England too. But candidates commonly present themselves to electorates as likeable, at the least. What would that impulse do to the requirement, established by other pressures, that bishops should have the unlikeable qualities of efficient managers?

The election of bishops anywhere is indirect at best. The electorate is limited and serious-minded. It commands more information about a candidate's performance in previous posts, and knows better how to read it, than a mass electorate possibly could. All methods of choosing people are fallible, especially when evidence from the past is only partly relevant, since people are being examined on their suitability for work they have not so far done. But limited election is as little fallible a method as any. It samples as wide a range of knowledge as possible, short of including the know-nothing vote. It has its own internal balances. It is if anything less likely to be bamboozled, better armoured against mere charm, than a smaller group of selectors.

In the Church of England, bishops are now in effect chosen by the Crown Appointments Commission. That is to say, the name the prime minister sends to the monarch, and the monarch to the dean and chapter of the vacant see, is no longer found by the prime minister on the advice of the Downing Street staff: since 1977, it is one of a pair of names sent to Downing Street by the chairman of a commission of twelve members of the Church of England, part clerical and part lay. (On a couple of occasions since 1981 Mrs Thatcher has forwarded to the Queen the second name of the pair, which was the name the commission liked only second best. That was still well within the terms of the 1976 agreement between Downing Street, Buckingham Palace and Lambeth Palace.)

But this already is indirect election, in miniature. The chair at the Crown Appointments Commission is taken by the Archbishop of Canterbury, with the Archbishop of York in support; and no one has elected them, true. Four more members, though, come from the diocese in need of a bishop: however the four are chosen, there are the dawnings of local choice here. And the other six members come from the Church of England's General Synod: three from its House of Clergy, three from its House of Laity. They have themselves been elected to the Synod: the clergy by most of their fellow clergy, the laypeople by a sample electorate of deanery synods; and thence elected by the Synod to the Commission. There, all twelve serve as an electorate themselves. Set against the million or so regular churchgoers of the Church of England, to say nothing of the much larger number that occasionally uses its services, the element of representative choice is tiny; but it is there.

It is at present modified by other things besides numbers. One modifier is the preponderant influence enjoyed by the two archbishops, and especially by the Archbishop of Canterbury. In the chair, the holder of that office brings to bear both ancient rank and personal fame. The Archbishop may well be in the job a decade, whereas the General Synod contingent must step down after five years, and the people from the waiting diocese are up from the country on a day return. A shrewd Archbishop will have concerted a line with the other professional of comparable dignity, the Archbishop of York. All in all, the Lambeth candidate will be very difficult for the rest of the Commission to stop. The present Archbishop of Canterbury is in a position to exert more influence on episcopal appointments than any of his predecessors since the office was instituted in 597.

This vantage has been noticed. The Bishop of Chichester, Eric Kemp, writing from the Church of England's Catholic wing, proposed in the summer of 1987 that the two Archbishops should be removed from the Commission altogether. Then the voice of the diocese and its churchmanship would be more loudly heard. The fear in the minds of critics is always that bishops as a group will become too like one another, leaving no room for departures from the orthodoxy of the time.

A further observation can be used to heighten the same fear, and again to modify the idea that the Church of England already operates a system of election. More than half the diocesan bishops now in place were suffragan bishops first. Of the forty-one diocesans known to the *Church of England Year Book* when its 1987 edition went to press, twenty-two had been suffragans. Of the thirty-one of those diocesans chosen after 1977, when the Crown Appointments Commission began functioning, seventeen had been suffragans. There is nothing troublesome about that, on the face of it. These were men promoted to the higher level for the unimpeachable reason that they had done well at the lower. But another consideration intrudes. These were also men who had been chosen as suffragans by a diocesan acting alone, as is effectively a diocesan's right. In other words, more diocesans than not are chosen from a slate of candidates compiled by all the other diocesans and by no one else. If a body of like-minded people wanted to make sure they stayed like-minded, this would be a good way to arrange things. It looks more like co-option than election.

It is fair to add that the list of names bruited about as of people who ought to have become bishops and have not is very short; and some of them have been offered the elevation and declined it. The fact remains that the movement of ideas in the Church of England, and the example of the rest of Anglicanism, makes the present system look unappealingly closed. Since it has been in operation barely ten years, rapid reform should not be expected; but before the end of the century the membership of the Crown Appointments Commission may well be progressively altered and enlarged, and its powers extended to cover the appointment of suffragans.

If the Commission were enlarged, it would lose one of its present properties, which is that it is astonishingly discreet. There are few parallels for the tightness of its discipline. In ten years, journalists have had almost no success in discovering who else was considered and rejected. An enlarged body could not be expected to keep the same silence. Yet that would not be a heavy loss. In other provinces of Anglicanism the names of the unsuccessful are known without their appearing to suffer for it. It is a commonplace of secular elections that the names of candidates are published. In an election for bishop, to be entered as a candidate at all would be an honour. Discretion is an over-valued virtue in English public life.

An enlarged Commission with an increased remit could still observe the same constitutional conventions. The

Commission's chairman could still nominally be advising the prime minister on how to advise the monarch. Establishment, the Church of England's special relationship with the Crown in Parliament, need not be affected. It is true that current arrangements for bishop-making can give no special satisfaction to the present Queen. Queen Victoria interested herself closely in the names put up to her for Church preferment, sometimes vetoing them. Her influence was on the whole benign. She helped take secular politics out of bishop-making. Queen Elizabeth II cannot even usefully discuss the names with her prime minister: the real decisions have already been taken. This may perhaps be a loss. The present Queen, like her great-great-grandmother, is knowledgeable in Church affairs. But her successors may not be. The process of change in establishment is now too far gone to stop.

6

Establishment

Just as there is a handful of 'royal peculiars' within the Church of England, where the Crown has special rights, so the Church of England itself is the royal peculiar within Anglicanism. The Church of Scotland maintains a connection with the Crown, of an unrestrictive kind, but the Church of Scotland is Presbyterian. Anglicanism in Ireland (including Northern Ireland) and Wales had the Crown links cut in 1871 and 1920. In the Anglican Communion, establishment is unique to England.

Its being so much an anomaly might suggest that it is due to disappear there too. But anomalies have been durable in English public life, and of late years establishment has been under little attack. It has lost much of its power to annoy. Perhaps its likeliest fate is to fade away so gradually that there will never be an identifiable moment when it can be pronounced gone.

There has been mutual help between Church and State in Europe ever since Constantine bestowed the imperial favour on Christianity in the fourth century. Roman missionaries in the sixth and seventh centuries would have made little ground in pagan England without the consent of Anglo-Saxon kings. For its part, the Church repeatedly came to the aid of the medieval English State by asserting the divine prerogatives of kings. In Tudor times, when the Church of England arrived more or less at its modern form, Church and State were conterminous: the whole nation was notionally a single Christian society, run by a Christian monarch under God. It was not a notion which the Bible-venerating Reformers had found in the New Testament: it had more to do with their rejecting the international political claims of the medieval papacy. But it did at any rate give coherence to a state of affairs where the Crown appointed the bishops, who then served the Crown in Parliament, while the law prescribed what services every church was to use, which then became the only legal services. They included the services for christenings, weddings and burials.

There are things about establishment that many English people value. They like the fact that baptism and marriage and funeral services in parish churches, though no longer inescapable, are still (with certain provisos) universally available. They like the fact that senior churchpeople are seen and heard in top places, crowning the monarch, piping up in the Lords, saying prayers at the Cenotaph, putting in a public word for God. Belief seems in some way authenticated if it is taken seriously in these surroundings. More generally, many English people like belonging to a country that has a national Church at all. Its mere existence suggests that the State they find themselves members of does ultimately look to moral and not just pragmatic standards.

These are comfortable persuasions, and they explain why the Church of England is unlikely ever to advocate disestablishment as a single deliberate act. But they are gradually losing their force. General Church of England provision of the rites of passage will tail away. In certain places, part-time ministries will make it impossible: a minister will not always be on hand when wanted. In others, incumbents are already more and more unwilling to dispense baptisms and weddings to parents and couples who show no other discernible Christian interest. (Evangelical reluctance over indiscriminate baptism is documented in the third chapter of Michael Saward's book.) The services of a minister for all comers at crematorium chapels are supplied by local churches acting together, not by the Church of England alone.

The Church of England's presence in places of power, next, is already partly shared. At big national occasions like coronations and memorial services and royal weddings, the Cardinal Archbishop of Westminster and the Moderator of the Free Church Federal Council are carefully built in to the proceedings alongside the Archbishop of Canterbury. This is more than a proper courtesy to the English Christians they represent: it also indicates that the decision to give these ceremonies a religious form follows not from the special position of the Church of England but from a perception that the country has many Christians in it. Roman Catholicism and the Free Churches are there even though they are not established; the Church of England would still be there even if it were not established.

The top place where the Church of England is most visibly present is the House of Lords. The Church of England is there in force: both archbishops and the three senior bishops (London, Durham and Winchester) are members by right, and another twenty-one bishops by seniority in the job. A duty bishop says prayers at the beginning of each afternoon's business, to a thin house. There is some benefit to the Church of England in this presence. On the huge range of topics the Lords discusses, a Church of England view can be put forward. It is sometimes based on sound local knowledge. On the dismantling of metropolitan councils, and on competition in local bus services, it helped change the detail of recent legislation. In one rousing incident in 1986 the bishops were on the winning side when the Government lost a bill to lift the restrictions on Sunday shopping. But the bill was in fact killed in the Commons. When the bishops are not in coalition with secular forces, they can achieve little. They had no success with their brief resistance to easy divorce.

If the advantages of this presence in the Lords are not striking, neither are the disadvantages. It may inhibit outspoken episcopal criticism of the Government of the day. But the inhibition is not that the bishops find themselves caught in the golden cage of privilege, and are therefore unwilling to rattle the bars too hard for fear of being put outside. The real inhibition, as the Archbishop of York testifies in the chapter on establishment in *Church and Nation in a Secular Age*, is knowledge. Once you are close to the seats of power, you begin to understand how difficult its exercise is: how circumscribed are the choices open to it, and how attended with problems they all are. That may not be a bad thing. For pulpiteering it can substitute hard thought.

Another questionable consequence of bishops in the Lords is the continuing Government influence in their appointment. When the Crown Appointments Commission was agreed in 1976 the then Prime Minister, James Callaghan, made no bones about his view that if bishops were still to sit in the Lords they could not be chosen by the Commission with unfettered freedom: Downing Street, which chooses or approves all other new peers, would have to retain the power of choosing between the two proffered names, and even vetoing them both. But in fact in ten years the right not to take the top name has been used only twice, and the veto never; and no worthy *episcopabili* appear to have had their names withheld because the Commission feared being crossed. The more important problem about the choosing of bishops is the narrowness of the Commission's own membership.

No: the fatal flaw about the heavy Church of England presence in the Lords, and the thing that will bring it to an end, is that it is unfair to other Churches. The Lords is the upper house of a Parliament that rules the whole of the United Kingdom. The Church of England is not the only established Church in the United Kingdom: there is also the Church of Scotland. It is not even the only Anglican Church: there is also the Scottish Episcopal Church, the Church in Wales, and the Church of Ireland. It is by no means the only large body of Christian believers: there are also the Nonconformists and the Roman Catholics. Yet the Church of England has twenty-six of its clerics in the Lords as a matter of right, and none of those other Churches have any at all. (In 1987 there happened also to be a Methodist minister and one from the Church of Scotland, Lord Soper and Lord MacLeod of Fuinary; but they were both very old, and their Churches had no rights about replacing them when they died.)

This unfairness is now hard to defend, and a diminishing number of Church of England people would seek to defend it. If professional churchpeople are worth hearing in the Lords at all, they should represent their profession as it exists throughout the United Kingdom. If all the professionals outside the Church of England are not worth hearing, then neither are those in the Church of England.

The problem has been canvassed for some while. The non-radical solution is to reduce the size of the Church of England contingent. The Wilson Government's proposals for Lords reform in 1968 contemplated cutting the number of bishops by ten, to sixteen. But that would have been only to make the problem less gross, not to solve it. Those proposals failed, as systematic attempts at Lords reform generally will; and there seems at present to be little impetus towards it. It is much more likely to go on happening bit by bit, as it has since the introduction of life peers earlier in the 1960s. This gradualism could still accommodate the radical solution. That would be to abolish the Church of England's present rights in the Lords altogether.

Instead, a much diminished number of Church of England bishops would sit as life peers. So too would a number of Free Church leaders, and so would a number of Roman Catholic bishops, if the Pope could allow an exception to his ban on Roman Catholic clerics as members of political assemblies. These new life peers would be chosen in just the same way as existing life peers: by the prime minister, on the advice of the Downing Street staff, after consultation with the leaders of the interests concerned. Those denominational leaders would themselves have held such consultations as they thought fit. The Lords is not an elected chamber.

The numbers, in the first instance, might be eight Anglican bishops (to include, from time to time, leaders of the other three Anglican Churches wholly or partly in the United Kingdom); four senior ministers of the Free Churches (including the Church of Scotland); and four Roman Catholic bishops (again with a geographical spread). These numbers are small, and might later be added to; but even at their initial level they could still be effective, because the new peers spiritual would be peers for life.

At present, bishops serve in the Lords under a disadvantage peculiar to themselves. While they are there they also have to run a diocese, which keeps them extremely busy; and as soon as they retire from their diocese they have to retire from the Lords. Yet after their retirement they remain bishops, just as a retired Free Church minister remains a minister; and they retain their faculties, and have more time to exercise them than before. Every few years a bishop's departure leaves a real sense of loss in the Lords. It is a chamber that thrives on the wisdom and urbanity of age. If bishops could stay there after retirement (as Free Church ministers already can), they could devote their main energies to the work, keeping in close touch both with Lords business and with Church opinion. Fewer of them than now could do a better job. And the Anglican bishops' presence would be proportionate to their weight in the community at large, and in decent relation with the standing of other Churches.

Such a reform might well have the side effect of allowing Downing Street to lift its hand from the appointment of Church of England bishops, and to let a single name from the Crown Appointments Commission go straight through to the monarch. It might also have another side effect. Parliament as a whole, Lords and Commons, still keeps ultimate control of the Church of England's internal legislation. Measures passed by the General Synod – about clergy housing, or the amalgamation of parishes, or appropriate ages for retirement – must go to Parliament for final approval, and thence for royal assent. Along with the Downing Street veto on bishops, it is the reverse side of establishment: national privileges require national control. But the main national privilege left to the Church of England is bishops in the Lords as of right. Take that away, and the case for residual parliamentary control would be further weakened.

The control itself dates from the provision by Elizabeth I that uniformity of Church practice should be enforced by the law of the land. Its modern justification is that the Church of England is the Church of the whole people of England, or at any rate of all those people in England who are not identifiably members of any other Church; that Parliament, and in particular the Commons, represents the whole people of England as accurately as is possible, and certainly more accurately than the General Synod does, with its narrow electorate; and that Parliament is therefore right to keep an eye on the General Synod's doings to see that the interests of plain people in pews are not run away with by wild eyed activists.

The practical problem about this theoretical justification is that most members of Parliament, in both houses, are now indifferent to Christianity in any form. Among those who are not, the total of Roman Catholics, Free Church people (including members of the Church of Scotland) and non-English Anglicans would probably outweigh the total of Church of England supporters. Nowadays the number of interested Church of England people in each house would not be more than a few dozen. Among them, traditionalists preponderate, weighting the parliamentary judgement of Church affairs in favour of the old way of doing things. Certainly there is a risk, in a Church which keeps its doors open for a large body of only occasional attenders, that these casuals will end by being ill served because the regulars have moved too far ahead of them. But Parliament is no longer the instrument to keep that risk in check.

Part of the parliamentary control over the General Synod has already been given up. In the Worship and Doctrine Measure 1974, Parliament approved a proposal from the General Synod that the Synod should have unsupervised charge of the forms in which the Church of England worshipped and the ways in which its doctrines were regulated. It was an act of piecemeal disestablishment; and this is the way disestablishment is likely to proceed. Relations between the Synod and the diminishing group of interested parliamentarians are now always potentially ill-tempered. Most Synod members think the parliamentarians ignorantly reactionary, and the parliamentarians think most Synod members foolishly given to change. Each side believes that the other abuses its power. Every now and again the parliamentarians take such action as they find open to them. Measures from the Synod are kept waiting an unreasonable length of time for parliamentary approval. On one occasion in 1984, incensed by plain speaking about doctrine from the new Bishop of Durham, the parliamentarians contrived to throw a Synod measure out altogether. It was innocent enough: it was a proposal to save money and time, and serve truth, by abolishing that part of the bishop-making process which requires that after bishops have been appointed by the Crown they should be elected by their new cathedral chapter; but the measure was taken to symbolize meddling modernism, and it went. In due time, if this kind of intervention goes on, a sufficient number of disinterested MPs will perceive that it is unfair as well as unedifying, since it involves the pursuit of private grievances through public channels. If the General Synod then asks to be given full charge of a further slice of its affairs, or even all of them, Parliament will grant its request. If, on the other hand, fearing this, the interested parliamentarians withhold their opposition to Synod measures, then parliamentary approval will become automatic and parliamentary control a dead letter. Either way, there will have been a further move in the process of gradual disestablishment.

The final element in establishment that people value, besides the offer of rites of passage to all comers and the presence of Church leaders in high places, is the sense that a nation with an established Church is somehow a moral nation. But this is surely an illusion. If the claim is that the existence of an established Church bears witness to the existence of other standards of conduct besides the material or expedient, then many citizens would answer that they hardly need the whole rigmarole of bishops intervening in Parliament and Parliament intervening in the affairs of the Church to tell them that. Some of them might also bridle at the easy identification of morality with religion. If the claim is that an established Church, witnessing to moral standards, actually makes those standards more faithfully observed than they would otherwise be, then the claim looks plainly untrue. It credits the Church of England with a power that even its most admiring supporters would hardly ascribe to it: the power of lessening human selfishness and cruelty more effectively than any other Church or any other set of moralists. Ordinary observation suggests that the level of public and private morality in England is much what it is in neighbouring countries unblest with an established Church: in some things higher, in some things lower. It would be very difficult to demonstrate that behaviour had worsened in Ireland since 1871 or in Wales since 1920, the dates when the Anglican Church was disestablished in those countries. It was not a majority Church in either country, true; but neither is it now in England. In sum, it will not be an argument based on national morality that deserves to save establishment in England from the slow disappearance that awaits it.

7

Politics

Bishops in the Lords suggests the Church in politics. That idea at once creates a tension. Christians find in themselves an instinctive sense that Christian political activism is both fitting and unfitting. There is a political churchman in *Richard II*: the Bishop of Carlisle. Shakespeare, who found him in Holinshed's *Chronicles* but built up the bishop's part, makes him an early Nonjuror. When his fellow peers hail Bolingbroke as Henry IV, the bishop declares that Richard is still God's 'captain, steward, deputy-elect', and that to depose him is treason. (The bishop also serves the useful dramatic purpose of being able to say, in effect, 'Watch it: you're starting the Wars of the Roses.') As we follow the play, we admire this outspokenness on what the bishop considers a moral point. But when, at the end of the same scene, he becomes a militant political conspirator in support of it, we are alarmed for him: not just because he is certain to lose, but because we feel that he has stepped out of his proper ground; and we recognize at the end that, in a cruel age, he is lucky to get away with his life.

Among Anglicans, who are Christians of the head as well as the heart, this tension will persist. Some of them will always be in politics, and some of them – sometimes the same people – will wonder whether they ought to be. Quietism will endure alongside activism.

It has been so in the past. One of the most heartening passages in the Church of England's history has been the story of its intellectual and practical concern, starting in the middle of the nineteenth century, for the problems of the poor; particularly, though not exclusively, in the East End of London. Something of the story is told in chapter eight of Francis Penhale's book on Anglican Catholics. Charles Kingsley, to take an instance, was the political parson at all points. He instituted a shoe club and a coal club for his Hampshire parishioners even before he instituted confirmation classes. As Parson Lot, in a short-lived journal called *Politics for the People* that his associates Frederick Denison Maurice and John Malcolm Ludlow edited during 1848, he declared that the Bible was a book written to keep the rich, not the poor, in order; he wrote both a pamphlet (*Cheap Clothes and Nasty*) and a novel (*Alton Locke*) which could leave the polite world in no doubt of the miseries endured by the garment workers who kept it clothed; as a visiting preacher in a West End church he said that all systems of society which favoured the accumulation of capital in a few hands were contrary to the kingdom of God, and he was repudiated at the end of the service by the vicar, much to the interest of the national press. (There is a typically vivid and scrupulous account of the incident in the fifth chapter of the first part of Owen Chadwick's history of *The Victorian Church*.)

Kingsley later drew back from parts of his radicalism; but he and his friends had their effect. The slum priests who ennoble the record of the Church of England from the 1850s onward were partly in the East End because their ritualistic tastes in worship made it difficult for them to get work elsewhere. But they were also there because they were encouraged by people and ideas that Kingsley had inspired; and they stayed, and laboured for their people's material as well as moral well-being, and founded a tradition that has remained lively to this day.

Yet Augustus Hare, to take another instance, had been ministering to his Wiltshire parish not long before in a very different spirit; and he too was followed by many later examples. He was as high-minded a cleric as Kingsley. Hare gave up the teaching of philosophy at New College, Oxford, to spend the last few years of his life as rector of the small college living of Alton Barnes, before he died in his forties of tuberculosis. His parishioners were farm-workers and their families. He is chiefly known from a book compiled by his nephew and namesake, *Memorials of a Quiet Life*: the quiet life in question was lived by the rector's wife, Maria. The two of them were not indifferent to the trials of the poor. In the rectory barn they ran a weekly clothes and materials shop which they subsidized heavily out of their own pockets, and gave suppers for the old people of the village, whom the rector waited on himself. But in the agitations across southern England in the winter of 1830 for a decent agricultural wage, Hare was an uncompromising defender of the property rights of the local landowning farmers. His dominant concern was to urge the Christian life and the Christian hope; and it would be impossible to say that he did not preach them and exemplify them effectively, and lessen much individual unhappiness along the way. Where Kingsley was a Christian activist, Hare was a Christian quietist.

These two sharply different responses to the problem of avoidable evil seem bound to continue within Anglicanism, since both of them can be defended by recourse to scripture, tradition and reason. Jesus, as far as we know from the scriptural record, taught both an equal regard for every human creature and an indifference to material well-being. The first justifies the Kingsley approach, the second the Hare. It will continue to be argued against Christians of the Kingsley persuasion that they are entitled to enunciate a general principle like the equal value of every human being, but not to stray into suggestions about how best to honour that principle: not to say that it requires the spending of extra public money on housing, for example, or on public works to produce jobs, since those particular measures may have the opposite effect. They may have the effect of pulling everyone down into an economic depression where no one's worth can be properly realized.

That argument will not silence Christian political recommendations, nor does it deserve to. It suggests that a principle can be separated from its application. In fact, though, a principle can be intelligibly stated only in its application. Otherwise it floats free, unattached to human experience. It cannot be seen to be applicable unless the application is examined. This distinction between principle and application is in fact a claim that politics should be left to politicians. But that is not a statement of the same order as that flying airliners should be left to airline pilots. It posits a degree of expertise in politicians as a class that is not borne out by their performance; nor could it be. Politics is an inexact science of vast range, dealing constantly with the hitherto unknown. In a properly run democracy it calls on the best thoughts of every citizen. All those citizens who offer their thoughts, professional clerics or even professional politicians, certainly run a risk of saying unwise or impractical things. But then they will be told so by someone who knows better, and may rephrase their thought, and out of the exchange a sound idea may emerge.

When politicians say that the clergy should stay out of politics, what they are perhaps saying is that they do not care to have the political argument invaded by anyone purporting to speak with a higher authority than their own, namely God's. But that is not what is happening. If clerics who talked politics did indeed claim to deliver the opinions of God, they would have a duty to do it unceasingly, in order to keep up with the unremitting output of decision demanded of national or local government; and if their claim were believed, the business of government would become awkward in the extreme, since ministers and councillors and officials would have to wait for each delivery of opinion, like Roman senators hanging about for the augurs to read the entrails of the sacrificial chicken. Happily, sensible clerics do not make any such claim; and if they did they could be identified, and put out of consideration, as not being sensible. No one knows the mind of God. The most that clerics are doing when they talk politics seriously is taking certain principles which they find in scripture, or to a lesser extent in the Christian tradition, and trying to apply them by a process of reason to the political problem in hand. This can be helpful to politicians, since it brings to bear a set of standards which politicians, rightly preoccupied with economics and public opinion, cannot have in the front of their minds. But if they think that the principles quoted at them are misunderstood, or inapplicable, or misapplied, they have only to say so. A clerical opinion is not the end of the argument.

Just as scripture, and in particular the teaching of Jesus, will support both an activist and a quietist attitude to politics, so will the tradition. It admits both social idealism and a conviction of human unreformability. It is, if you like, both semi-Pelagian and Augustinian.

Pelagianism, or a corruption of it, is the besetting heresy of the Left in politics: the belief that all human miseries can be removed by institutional reform, since human wickedness has no part in causing them: there would be no theft or prostitution if only everyone were assured of enough to live on. The besetting heresy of the Right is anti-Pelagianism: the belief that all human institutions will anyway be spoilt by human selfishness, so the only sensible thing to do is keep it as much in check as possible in whatever institutions you find yourself operating, and not bother to reform them: even slavery was benign in the United States. The sloganeer of anti-Pelagianism was Pope: 'For forms of government let fools contest; Whate'er is best administered is best.'

Social idealism, the quest for the city of God on earth, has figured constantly in the Christian tradition. Even Calvin, convinced as he was of human depravity, sought to set up a theocratic regime in Geneva. Monasticism kept the ideal of the perfect human community alive for centuries, and has been revived in the West in this century. Anglicanism has its part in these inheritances. Over against them stands the great Christian perception of original sin: that human beings can do nothing right, and human existence is not to be justified without forgiveness. Devised by a line of the Fathers from St Irenaeus to St Augustine, and refined by the medieval Schoolmen, in its plain form it appeals in some degree to every Christian's sense of truth. Common sense tells us that neither notion, of human reformability or its opposite, can be entirely true. The skill, the impossible skill, is to perceive where and how, and how far, to apply each principle. But what is clearly true is that both ideas are part of the Christian tradition from a very early stage, and that Christians are to that extent licensed to be in political terms activist or quietist, on the Left or on the Right, or at any point of their choosing on the continuum in between. Anglicans can be expected to go on making full use of this licence in the future.

Reason, finally, tells us that all creatures strive to improve their lot, that among human beings this is best done in concert, that the name of that activity is politics, and that there is thus a good case for engaging in it. Reason also tells us, though, that many of the improvements thus sought are of doubtful worth, and that human contentment is better secured by the limiting of wants than by the enlarging of them. Those simple syllogisms will justify anybody either in embracing political activity or in eschewing it. Christians add a second pair of arguments. If God loved the world enough to come and save it, then nothing that happens in the world need be presumed to be outside the divine interest, and the attempt to improve the way the tiniest part of it works is in line with the divine purposes. That argument is weakened for Christians who find they cannot in so many words accept the incarnation, but not destroyed: the idea of a loving God is enough to motivate a care for the world God loves. As against all that, if God's purpose in coming was to bring about a reconciliation between the human and the divine, then that reconciliation becomes the prime business of all Christians: their preoccupation ought to be their relation with their God; and even if they are non-incarnationists, a belief in the divine forgiveness would make them chiefly concerned to be as little undeserving of it in their own lives as they could.

Prediction about Anglicans and politics is thus not difficult. Invited by scripture, tradition and reason to be both activists and quietists, Kingsleys and Hares, some of them will choose one tendency and some the other. The elasticity of Anglicanism will contain both. Nor is it hard to foresee which tendency will preponderate. There will be flashes of activism. There was one such from a group of eight Church of England bishops with mainly urban responsibilities (six diocesans and two suffragans) at the beginning of the United Kingdom general election campaign in the summer of 1987. They publicized a list of questions on homelessness, unemployment and so on which voters might put to their parliamentary candidates; and the drift of the questions was unfriendly to the retiring (and later re-elected) Conservative Government, though the bishops refused to acknowledge as much. But in general there can be little doubt that the political choice of the mass of

Anglicans will be for quietism.

The evidence for that conclusion is partly in the past. Although not unique, Kingsley was untypical. There has been Christian political radicalism in England, but comparatively little of the inspiration has come from within the Church of England. Cromwell and Milton were Independents: Nonconformity supplied most of the people who fought and argued on the parliamentary side in the Civil War. It was Nonconformists who perceived that, if all human beings were indeed of equal worth in the sight of God, then the principle had a political bearing: there was Nonconformist pressure behind the Great Reform Bill and the setting up of trade unions. Most of the first Labour MPs were Nonconformists. When the Liberal Party was a force for reform, it drew its strength from the Nonconformist conscience.

In this century, the United Kingdom has not been one of those countries where the only effective opponents of the ruling regime have been churchpeople; and it shows no sign of becoming one, however much the power of the parliamentary Opposition to require government by national consensus may have dwindled under the Conservative Governments of the 1980s. Even in Northern Ireland, the active representatives of the Roman Catholic minority have been Sinn Fein and the Irish Republican Army, not the Roman Catholic Church. But it is the Roman Catholic Church in Poland that has stood for national consciousness under successive invaders, and will outlive the trade union Solidarity in that function under the Russians. Roman Catholic priests and thinkers in many South American and Central American countries have furnished the poor with a belief in the possibility of self-betterment, and a support against the cruelties of life and officialdom, that Governments have not been able or willing to supply. This is not a task that modern Protestantism, or Anglicanism, often finds itself discharging.

In Western Europe and North America, it is Roman Catholicism that consistently opposes Governments when they relax old restraints on divorce, abortion and the practice of homosexuality. Anglicanism, more sensitive than Roman Catholicism to the harshness of these restraints in the individual case and less to their usefulness in strengthening the resolve of society at large, has been found as often as not on the Government's side. When Garret FitzGerald, as Prime Minister of the Republic of Ireland, sought permission in successive referendums in 1983 and 1986 for abortion and divorce laws in the Republic where none had been before, and fell foul of the Irish Roman Catholic bishops in the attempt, he had the support of the bishops of the Church of Ireland.

For the future, it is hard to see Anglican leaders in sustained conflict with their Governments about anything. Consider two specimen political issues with a clear religious content.

One is nuclear disarmament. Despite progress being apparently made in it in the late 1980s by the great powers, the danger of nuclear war is at least as acute as ever, because of the number of smaller powers and even terrorist organizations that may attain nuclear weaponry. The case for pacifism, for a renunciation of all force, is stronger here than in any other kind of conflict, because any use of nuclear weapons would be a disaster. The power of pacifism is merely exemplary. Wars are not stopped by gestures; they are stopped by negotiation between Governments. But pacifism reminds Governments and their electors that wars are uniquely dreadful, licensing and magnifying all other evils; and pacifists reinforce this reminder by showing themselves ready to make any sacrifice of comfort or even life in pursuit of changes of heart that will save the rest of humanity. Because peacemakers are blessed in the Sermon on the Mount, and because the self-sacrificial love in pacifism can itself be Christlike, there has always been a strong Christian element in pacifism's development.

The denomination that has done most for pacifism in England and the United States has been the Quakers. The Anglican contribution has been thin; sometimes hostile, as Church of England attitudes were to conscientious objectors in the First World War. In gatherings both of the Church of England and of the Scottish Episcopal Church there was a flurry of interest in pacifist motions in the early 1980s; but it has fallen away again since. It is true that scripture, tradition and reason can all be read in both senses on the pacifist question. But here has been an issue of huge moment where a

Christian witness can have special point and weight; and Anglicanism has in the main not taken the issue up, preferring the argument that these are complex affairs best left to the professionals. The record does not suggest that a change of attitude impends.

The other test case, globally trivial and yet a continuing occasion of shame to several parts of the Christian community in the West, is Northern Ireland. The present phase of the troubles there has gone on since 1969. It is a sporadic guerrilla struggle between two tribes each aspiring to exclusive influence in the same six counties; and the two tribes wear Christian badges. Anglicanism has a special interest. Church of England bishops contribute with their presence, and many Church of England adherents with their votes, to the United Kingdom Parliament that carries political responsibility for the problem; and the Church of Ireland is one of the main denominations wearing the Protestant badge. But Anglican leaders have said little to the purpose about how the conflict might be ended, for the sufficient reason that they have not known what to say.

They might have tried saying this. The problem is in distant origin colonial; and in the modern world nearly all such problems have been regulated for good or ill by the departure of some of the colonist stock, with their armed backers from the mother country, and the absorption of the rest of it into the population that was there before it. Only then has the fighting stopped. On that reading, it is members of the Protestant tribe – the Anglican side – who would be well advised to prepare for departure or absorption. There would be Christian self-abnegation in the decision; there would also be prudence, since unless one tribe or the other softens its exclusive claims those six counties will never be at peace.

But it has not been said, and it is unlikely to be. Anglican leaders are too well aware that the Protestant tribe, thus advised, would not consent, resting on its local superiority in numbers, and might only make life more difficult than before for its clerical as well as its political guardians. Once again, the question is remitted to the experts.

Anglicans will never be political activists in any numbers.

They incline to trust Governments instead. Partly that inclination follows from the historic connection of the Church of England with the English governing classes, and thence with the armed forces of the Crown. The inclination may sometimes have been exported, by imperialists or missionaries, to reappear in Anglicanism elsewhere in the world. Partly it follows from the reasonableness of Anglicans, shading off into pragmatism. They know that nations and tribes take a long time to change their ways, to give up their belligerence, to renounce their ancestral claims. Anglicanism can contain political activists, but it does not readily attract or breed them. It is less likely to be radical politically than theologically. Theological radicalism has grown out of doctrinal tolerance, lay influence and academic freedom. Those qualities have had no comparable bearing on political attitudes.

8

Internationalism

Whether or not Anglicanism seeks to exert political influence internationally, it is an international communion. Its geographical extent is enormous. Two thirds of its provinces are in the Third World. Yet its numbers are not large. It claims seventy million adherents, grouped in four hundred and thirty dioceses: only ten times the number of dioceses that serve England and the Isle of Man. The spread is thin. The cost, in effort and money, of maintaining any genuine unity in it will not be negligible.

The value of unity, therefore, is worth casting up. Considered in certain lights, it is low. In part, Anglicanism is no more than a ghostly survival of the British empire. Empire was itself a transient and unthought phase in the history of Europe; it was a by-product of war, surplus population, competition for raw materials, competition for markets, national pride and national idealism. The other recruiting agent for Anglicanism was mission, at first from the United Kingdom, later from elsewhere: without it there could have been no Anglicanism in Brazil, China or Japan. But in the same period Roman Catholic and Lutheran and Free Church missionaries were equally active. The denomination of converts depended on who got to them first. Mission therefore had something of the same accidental quality as empire. There was thus no pre-existent identity of religious disposition which Anglicanism arrived to recognise. The different people who bear the same religious name are gathered under it as a matter of historical chance. There is nothing discreditable about that. In every country, many more churchgoers have had their Church chosen for them by the accidents of birth or upbringing or encounter or location than have chosen it themselves. But the origins of Anglican unity earn it no mystic reverence.

Moreover, unity is an insubstantial and fugitive concept for Anglicans, because it cannot mean unity of belief or practice. Anglicanism's wide geographical and cultural bounds make that kind of unity impossible. It is ruled out, too, by the explicit toleration of internal differences that has marked Anglicanism throughout its history. Unity across the Anglican Communion can mean no more than the unity of people who happen to be friends, not the unity of colleagues who think and act together.

There is nevertheless good to be extracted even from a unity that is haphazard in origin and undefined in practice. It is better than disunity. It diminishes the number of Christians from whom any one group of Anglicans need feel separated. It saves a little of the corporate energy that otherwise would in the past have been spent on inter-denominational controversy and would now be put into ecumenical discussion. It instigates a number of agreeable conferences, at Canterbury and elsewhere, at which Anglicans from many parts of the world can pray and think and even play cricket together; and although conferences have a way of influencing only the participants, and only for as long as they are conferring, strenuous efforts are made nowadays to include a broad range of people in the preceding local discussions. It forms part of the multiple modern machinery that enables individuals from widely separated countries to know one another in a little detail: a process which can do no harm to the cause of peace, and may do good.

If those were all the advantages, they would not be enough. But the international unity of Anglicanism can make higher claims than that. It is valuable as testimony and symbol. To the Christian world it shows that toleration works: great numbers of believers, having learned Christ in many different ways, would nevertheless rather think of themselves as worshipping together than as worshipping apart. To the secular world it makes the same point in more general terms: millions of people of different backgrounds and beliefs can co-exist. The fact of the Anglican Communion's solidarity can at need make a more directly political point than that. When the Church of the Province of South Africa, for example, is under threat, its membership of the Anglican Communion is one sign that it has friends overseas from whom it can expect moral and material support.

Internationally, then, the Anglican Communion stands for an important idea: the acceptance of diversity. Its size goes on increasing: the mere growth of population in the Third World sees to that. Its international visibility, therefore, is not likely to dwindle. Yet this comparative success itself raises certain questions.

The first is leadership. The Anglican Communion has the kind that matches its own dispersed and random growth. The Lambeth Conference, first held in 1867, happens every ten years or so. It assembles a few hundred bishops. For a long time this was held to be enough, supplemented by rare Pan-Anglican Congresses that brought in ordinary clergy and laypeople. The Lambeth Conference of 1968 established, in addition, an Anglican Consultative Council: it draws bishops, clergy and laity from the provinces, but in small numbers. The membership is something over sixty. The Council meets every two or three years, and its Standing Committee in the years between; its Secretary General (a Hawaiian in origin, Canon Samuel Van Culin) works from a base in London; it puts out information on Anglican affairs to journalists. To this the Lambeth Conference of 1978 added meetings, also every two or three years, of the Anglican primates, who number about ten. These groups discuss the structure of the Anglican Communion (whether to mark out new dioceses or provinces or regional councils); Anglicanism's relation to other Christian communions (through ecumenical conversation and the World Council of Churches); Christianity's relation to other faiths; and all the topics that churchpeople consider when they meet – what the faith is, how to propagate it, what its bearing is on the world's sorrows, and so on. None of this discussion binds other Anglicans, apart from the merely organizational part of it, and except in so far as they wish to be bound. It would be out of line with the permissiveness of Anglicanism, and with practicality, if it did.

This kind of leadership may be apt to Anglicanism as an idea. But it does not entirely fit with the way the world works.

International Anglicanism has remained obscure: not a secret, but not a familiar phenomenon, either. Anglicans themselves are chiefly aware of their own Church as a local or national presence. They are less conscious than they might be, less conscious than Roman Catholics are, of belonging to an international communion. To have the effect that it might, international Anglicanism would do well to become less obscure than it is. Journalists, expressing such public curiosity as exists, want to know what the organization thinks or intends, and where to apply to find out. Local Anglican leaders worldwide, observing the freedom with which Christian potentates travel in the 1980s, want to know whose presence will most clearly seal their celebrations and new beginnings with a sign that they belong in the larger whole. For those purposes, the Anglican Communion would profit from a direction of its affairs that was not distributed between four or five different bodies of shifting memberships, but gathered into a single standing organization with a permanent head.

Prediction is difficult here. These modern pressures may very well have their way. Yet such a change may do a certain violence to the genius of Anglicanism, and may deserve to be resisted on those grounds. The danger is of untruth. The Anglican Communion has never been the kind of organization that can be said at any moment to know what it thinks, because in different parts it thinks different things; and this is a gracious acceptance on its part of the facts of belief. A central body, therefore, that purported to speak with a single voice in its name might not be telling the truth about it. There is risk there, but risk which could be limited if the new leadership made scrupulous truthfulness its first consideration, to the point of invariably acknowledging disagreement if it existed.

Another possibility of untruth is more subtle. Much modern leadership involves deception. There is the letter from the minister which the minister has not written, but only signed; the prime minister's speech, delightedly applauded, which has in fact been put together by a civil servant or a party ghost-writer; the president's fireside chat on television, delivered without a note and as if from the heart, when every word is not only from another hand but also being read off a teleprompter.

In the political world, these things are regarded as the necessities of mass communication, and the element of fraud in them is discounted on the doubtful argument – doubtful in fact, doubtful morally – that 'everybody knows' they happen. In the world of the Christian Church they would fit less easily than that. It is one thing, and a perfectly proper thing, for Church leaders to consult someone else before they sit down to prepare a speech or a sermon; it would be quite another thing for them to pass off someone else's work as their own. Yet the declared leader of so large a body as the Anglican Communion would be beset with so many calls to speak and preach as to make that very hard to avoid. The risk could be in part overcome, again, by a rule of self-abasing honesty; in part, too, by refusing a high proportion of the opportunities offered. But those things are more easily said than done.

If these risks were overlooked or overcome, and such a leader appointed, it could not be the Archbishop of Canterbury. The holder of that office is already crushingly busy: he is leader of a lively and populous part of Anglicanism, and has special duties as such which it would be hard to shed – as diocesan bishop, as chairman of Church of England committees, as member of the Lords, as adviser to Government and Crown. The present Archbishop, Robert Runcie, might well not be succeeded by a figure of the same grace: a glance at the likely field of candidates suggests that the next Archbishop will be reflective rather than engaging. Archbishops of Canterbury are chosen with enormous care, through the machinery of the Crown Appointments Commission, to meet a particular set of requirements in England and the United Kingdom; not for their suitability for leading an international body, where different or extra qualifications might be needed, like a knowledge of languages or a readiness for constant travel. And Archbishops of Canterbury are not chosen by the Anglican Communion; as its leader must be, however indirectly. If Anglicanism is to be seen by outsiders and adherents as no longer the spiritual afterglow of the British empire, but as an international movement in its own right, it must one day go to some other source than the Church of England for its leadership. If the Roman Catholics can allow themselves to be led by a Pope who is not an Italian, and the United Nations by a Secretary General who is neither an American nor a Russian, and the World Council of Churches by a General Secretary who is not from one of the great Protestant communities of the West, then the Anglican Communion can admit a leader who is not from England.

The post thus created would be an upgraded version of the secretary-generalship of the Anglican Consultative Council. It would be upgraded, first, by an upgrading of the Council itself, so that, with an enlarged membership, it swept up all the functions of Lambeth Conferences and Pan-Anglican Congresses and primates' meetings into its own keeping. If the Lambeth Conference continued at all, it could be almost entirely recreational, to relieve at distant intervals the loneliness of the episcopal task. The remade Council would issue out of the whole of the Anglican Communion through some form of indirect election; and the members would themselves elect the new Secretary General. This servant of the whole Anglican Church would be given episcopal rank, if not already possessing it; would travel and write and speak as an elected leader, not as an appointed official; and would embody, for the time being, the voice and values of Anglicanism – uncertain voice and conflicting values though they would sometimes be.

Such a solution to the problem of Anglican leadership would produce an extra benefit. It would put an end to the question raised whenever a new Archbishop of Canterbury is to be appointed: namely, whether the new holder of the office ought not to be of some other origin than English. The idea is a bad one. The Archbishopric of Canterbury is embedded in the life of England, and to a lesser extent of the whole United Kingdom. To make the office work effectively, its holder needs a lifetime's understanding of how England works. A stranger could not command the necessary skill. The appointment would be fair neither to the stranger nor to the Church of England.

The present Archbishop has worked hard at international Anglicanism, visiting its distant provinces and its meetings and ceremonies in far places, helping to represent it at the World

Council of Churches, receiving its leaders and those of other Christian communions at Lambeth Palace. No change could be made before his likely retirement date in 1991. The next Archbishop, if a Secretary General of the new style were by then in place, would remain one of the most honoured figures in the Anglican Communion. The senior bishop of the country that began it all, the occupant of the see with which to be in communion is a sign of being an Anglican, could be nothing less. But those functions, and not the boundaries of the Anglican Communion itself, would mark the limit of the Archbishop's formal responsibilities.

It would be unwise to say that these things shall be. The most that can be said is that they have a strong logic about them.

Besides leadership, the other question raised by Anglicanism's internationalism is mission. Most Christian professionals still take it for granted that mission is to be admired and continued. They accept instructions like 'Go ye therefore, and teach all nations', at the end of St Matthew's Gospel, as neither a later addition to the sayings of Jesus nor a figure of speech. The optimism of the early years of this century, when Anglicans sang 'Nearer and nearer draws the time, the time that shall surely be, When the earth shall be filled with the glory of God as the waters cover the sea' and meant it, is modified now. But many of them still feel that Anglicanism in its international form, in particular, was helped in its growth by mission, and has no choice but to continue the missionary work.

It seems to me a safe prediction that by the early years of the twenty-first century this view will be openly losing its strength and persuasiveness, and Anglicanism will have come to be content with its accidental boundaries. Indeed, it is surprising that so much unargued missionary talk has survived thus far. The main era of European mission, between the Napoleonic Wars and the First World War, has by now been fairly well worked over by historians. It remains clearly true that many British missionaries to India, Africa and elsewhere fulfilled St Paul's injunction to the Christians at Corinth that they should be 'always bearing about in the body the dying of the Lord

Jesus'. They showed a sustained bravery and love of God in face of danger, hardship, disease and failure. They helped teach literacy, medicine, farming: the African generation that finally took power from the British in the 1960s is well known for having been mission-educated. They defended and explained their charges to the secular British power. But they needed the secular British power, and shared its assumptions of superiority over anything that life outside the European sphere could offer. They were part of an intruding culture which gave much, but also destroyed much. Undervaluing Indian and African religions, they interfered with a settled pattern of belief and conduct, but could not systematically replace it. Their converts were brought out of an old society and yet not furnished with a new one, or even with the equal society of Europeans. (A balance-sheet of this mixed achievement is well drawn up in chapter nine of the third volume of David L. Edwards's *Christian England*.)

In the world of commerce there is a notion that a business must be either expanding or contracting: there can be no point of rest. It is a notion that has no necessary application to the world of faith. Nothing obliges Anglicanism to push out its frontiers. Expansion is seldom into empty territory: it is nearly always at the expense of another occupancy, a rival system of belief. In an era when the West has been belatedly learning to respect non-Christian religions, and when Christians have been working towards an acceptance of each other's denominational divergences, and when Anglicans have begun to acknowledge the difficulties and problems of religious certainty, Anglicanism's residual missionary activity has an assertiveness about it that corresponds to no underlying truth.

Recognizing this, many Anglicans since the mid-1970s have redefined mission as covering any and every kind of church activity. By that means they can keep the name and abandon the thing named. Not everyone will consent even to that compromise. In Malaysia, Christians feel themselves threatened by legislation based on the Islamic legal code, the Shariah: that drinking alcohol in public should be punished with caning, for example. (The Government there says non-Muslims are exempt.) In Nigeria, Christians find themselves confronted by hostile Muslim rioters, though mosques as well as churches are burnt in the riots. In such circumstances Christians may persuade themselves that missionary attack is the best form of defence. But resentment against Christian missionary activity, from Jews and Hindus as well as Muslims, is by now sufficiently documented. Local aims may be served by such activity; international aims will not. Within Anglicanism as a whole, its inappositeness to the modern world is likely to be more and more widely perceived.

There is no long future, either, for the kind of missionary activity that reverses the old historical flow. The notion here is that Christians in Kenya or Papua New Guinea may have received or rediscovered a simpler, purer, more joyous Christianity than the form now current in world-weary Europe, and ought to bring it back to us as we once took ours to them. There was a good deal of talk in this sense in the 1970s and early 1980s, as a consequence of an initiative of the Anglican Consultative Council called Partners in Mission. This new kind of mission is no more reputable intellectually than the old kind. If the Christian West ought to respect the forms of belief, Christian and non-Christian, that exist in the developing world, so ought Christians from the developing world to respect the hesitations and coolnesses of Christianity in the West.

Intervention by new believers would anyway change nothing. There can be a legitimate difference of opinion about whether Western Christianity is growing old or growing up; but either way, the process of ageing is not reversible.

9

Ecumenism

Anglicanism is unlikely, then, to expand. There is another scenario for its future: that it will disappear. The disappearance would be a happy one: through the processes of ecumenism, Anglicanism would be absorbed into the single Great Church of the future.

Ecumenism is an old phenomenon. Gibbon (in the twenty-first chapter of the *Decline and Fall*) quotes and translates a passage about the state of fourth-century Christianity in the Roman empire during the reign following Constantine's. The passage is from the soldier and historian Ammianus. 'The highways were covered with troops of bishops galloping from every side to the assemblies, which they call synods; and while they laboured to reduce the whole sect to their own particular opinions, the public establishment of the posts was almost ruined by their hasty and repeated journeys.' Now that bishops are no longer entitled to free post-horses, but instead have to have their airfares paid by their Churches, the ecumenical process offers the travel business riches rather than ruin. That aside, the picture has altered little.

Christians have always pulled apart, and most of them have wished that they were together again, or at least that other Christians believed as they did. Within the Church of England, even in the days when it was secured as the one Church for all citizens by every persuasion of the law, the first declared division appeared hardly more than a hundred years after the Elizabethan settlement: on St Bartholomew's day, 1662, the day Charles II's new Act of Uniformity required of all parish ministers that they should accept a mildly high-church new Prayer Book and should be reordained if during the Puritan supremacy they had been ordained only by church elders, more than a thousand of them opted for dissent, though in so doing they lost their livelihood and were then pursued with prohibitions on free worship and personal advancement. Decent latitudinarians tried hard to bring these Bartholomeans back; but reordination in particular remained an affront to the Nonconformists, and Parliament was reluctant to indulge Protestant dissenters in a way that must also benefit Roman Catholics, who were under constant suspicion of making friends with the country's enemies.

The legal disabilities laid on both Protestant and Catholic dissenters have been gradually lifted. The obstacles to Christian reunion have remained. Another long sequence of efforts at the reunion of the Church of England with its Protestant allies began at the Lambeth Conference of 1920; and when it came to an end, with the collapse of the Anglican-Methodist scheme in 1972 and the covenanting scheme in 1982, the case was only slightly altered. The Church of England was still facing in two directions. There were still the Roman Catholics to be considered as well as the Free Churches. The difference this time was that, instead of seeming to objectors to be too friendly towards Roman Catholics, the proposals seemed too unfriendly. A significant minority of clerical and lay opinion in the Church of England would have preferred Catholic reunion to Protestant reunion, and were not prepared to accept the second if it endangered the first.

In the heyday of ecumenical optimism, which lasted from the 1920s to the 1970s, this facing-both-ways quality in the Church of England, and in Anglicanism generally, was held to be an advantage. If you drew a Venn diagram of institutional Church life, with a circle for the Catholic tradition and a circle for the Reformed, the lozenge-shaped area where they coincided was Anglicanism. In the preferred metaphor, Anglicanism had the capacity to become a bridge Church. But most bridges join only two pieces of land. In the detail of ecumenical negotiation it began to emerge that Anglicanism spanned many more than that. A Venn diagram that did justice to it would show a constellation of coinciding circles. This made life difficult for ecumenists from other, more single-minded communions. Since a part of Anglicanism could be found to agree with anybody, the whole of it could agree with nobody.

It is worth saying that there is nothing discreditable about disunity. It is as old as Christianity itself: witness St Paul's opening reproach to the Corinthians: 'Every one of you saith, I am of Paul; and I of Apollos; and I of Cephas; and I of Christ.' It is a fact of all religions: belief is both intensely personal, and therefore subject to all the variations of humanity, and intensely important, and therefore held in any particular form with a strength which regards any other form as an affront. Disunity is human. Samuel John Stone's hymn 'The Church's one foundation', written to support Bishop Gray of Cape Town when he sought to depose Bishop Colenso for heresy, and still sung, speaks of the 'scornful wonder' with which the world at large regards schisms and heresies within Christianity. The sentiment is in fact seldom heard except as a debating point. The journalist reporting church affairs, and having regularly to canvass secular views of them, encounters neither wonder nor scorn at Christian divisions. The secular world is well aware of differences in many other parts of human life: in politics, in sport, in science. People believe in democratic politics as a process without believing that only one political party is right about everything: indeed, if the system is to work properly there needs to be more than one in good standing. Scientists differ about the origins of the universe without science itself being brought into contempt. There is nothing about Christianity, as a system of belief, which alters the human character and lifts it above its normal tendency to disagreement. Indeed, part of the genius of Christianity is that it accepts the human character as it is, in all its individuality and fallibility: so far from being a system to make us good, it is a way of reconciling us to the fact that we are not good. Jesus is represented in St John as praying, of his future followers, 'that they all may be one'; and it is certainly impressive that the author of that Gospel took Christian unity seriously, and has been followed by many principled believers. But it has to be acknowledged that those believers have always been a minority. Scripture is comparatively laconic about disunity; the tradition is tolerant of it; reason suggests that Christians are more self-castigatory about it than they need be.

It goes without saying that if disunity is not discreditable, neither is the effort to end it. The idea of a single Great Church is a noble one. It does honour to the oneness of God. And although the search was doomed not to find the thing sought, the act of searching has done good. Aiming for the unattainable has increased the measure of the attainable. The years of negotiation between Anglicans and Free Church people, Anglicans and Lutherans, Anglicans and Roman Catholics, Anglicans and the Orthodox, have at least accustomed numbers of churchpeople to the idea that such dealings are respectable. In England the effect is most marked at the level of the ordinary parish. For generations it had been normal for Church of England clergy to treat their Free Church fellow ministers negligently; and where encounters were not to be avoided, as over Nonconformity's exercise of its right to burials in the graveyards of parish churches, the attitude of incumbents was grudging. It was one of the least attractive aspects of Anglicanism. It has almost gone. Where it survives, it is the exception, not the rule. With Roman Catholics there was hardly any contact at all. Church of England clergy were conscious of being regarded by them as not properly ordained, and took their revenge by regarding Roman Catholics as not properly English. The mutual ignorances are being steadily dispelled. Encouraged by the activity they saw among their national leaders, the denominations began in the 1960s and 1970s to work together locally; and when the national enterprise faltered, the local effort was often quickened to make up for it.

United services have become common, though they stop short of the eucharistic in order not to embarrass the Roman Catholics, whose Church still disallows any general invitation to other people to take communion at its altars. Local councils of churches abound. In many places, some or all of the local churches, sometimes including the Roman Catholics and sometimes not, bind themselves to do everything together that they are not obliged by the rules of their own communion to do separately. Church buildings are shared: a United Reformed Church congregation will worship late on a Sunday morning with the incense burnt by its Anglo-Catholic hosts still heavy in the air, and think nothing of it. Local charitable work is shared. Colleges of church origin for training teachers, theological colleges, university faculties of theology, will employ teachers of more than one denomination, as a matter of local decision. Local clergy make common pronouncements on matters of local concern. In Liverpool, the partnership for local purposes of the Roman Catholic archbishop with the Church of England bishop has become famous. In Scotland, this kind of enterprise has reached national level. Since 1980 a Church Leaders' Forum has met Government leaders once or twice a year to put forward views from within the Churches on problems like unemployment or the abuse of drugs. Originally a Government initiative, it groups nine different Churches.

The extent or effect of this movement should not be overstated. The bulk of church activity remains exclusively denominational. But these essays in unity happen, and they will continue to happen, and perhaps to increase. They represent the beginnings of the necessary, decent minimum of ecumenism: that churchpeople, and in particular church professionals, from different denominations should recognize one another as colleagues rather than rivals. Ordinary Christians have no need of organic and doctrinal unity between the Churches. They need practicalities. They need to be able to marry into another denomination than their own without conditions imposed. They need – in such a marriage, or when they are on holiday abroad, or simply out of Christian friendship – to be allowed to take communion at the altars of other denominations than their own. For the good of their own souls, they need the humble knowledge that their own denomination does not claim to be wholly and exclusively in the right.

As things are, the achievement of these simple things is made to wait on the outcome of a process that can have no outcome. Practical intercommunion, say the ecumenical specialists, must be deferred until there is doctrinal agreement on what intercommunion means. Yet that agreement, since an understanding of communion involves an understanding of everything else, will never come.

The key issue is authority. Where there is disagreement between two Christian communions, it will never be talked or negotiated away. It might if the communions were so small that all the members of both could fit round the same table. The friendliness of ecumenical discussion is notoriously contagious. The actual participants may well agree to think the same thing henceforward. But the moment the participants speak for others besides themselves, complications ensue. In a matter so personal and so profound as religion, different people will have varying views and will hold them strongly. Why should those people accept what their side in the negotiation has agreed to believe on their behalf? Because the high command of their Church tells them to. But what gives that high command the right to be obeyed: what text, what custom, what agreement?

Christian believers answer that question in many different ways; but the answers are in essence of two types. Some believers sit loose to all authority: they may respect many kinds, they may base themselves on a scripture or a formula, but in the end they give the highest place to their own private judgement. They reserve the right to decide for themselves. They exalt their own intellectual freedom. Others require authority. They may perceive the case for questioning it, and in secular affairs they may be very ready to; but in religion they prefer to be told where they may stand. They are prepared to subordinate their own judgement to the settled judgement of a great institution. They exalt intellectual certainty.

It is the Reformation divide. The Reformation was not just an unfortunate misunderstanding, a squabble over questions that have lost their interest: it identified the deepest single division in the human approach to religion. The Reformed interest is on the side of private judgement. There are upholders of the Reformed interest, especially on Anglicanism's Catholic wing, who are happy with the idea of authority as long as it can be satisfactorily defined. But they are awkwardly and untypically placed; as are intellectual libertarians within Roman Catholicism. The religious institution that exists to accommodate the desire for certainty in Christian belief is pre-eminently the Roman Catholic Church.

The genius of the Roman Catholic Church is to be both authoritarian and conservative. That is the secret of its matchless durability. There have been secular administrations that contrived to be authoritarian and revolutionary. But they have not lasted long. Roman Catholicism is too wise to put that degree of strain on the loyalty of its adherents. It seldom asks them to change their doctrinal or moral beliefs. And as reward for their loyalty it gives them a blessed deliverance from uncertainty. They are able to be sure that what they are asked to believe is true. For this they are offered the authority of their Church, declared on a certain reading of the New Testament to have been founded by Christ himself, and interpreted to the modern world by the Vicar of Christ on earth, the Pope.

Anglicans therefore face a number of problems in ecumenical discussion with Roman Catholicism. One is their own tendency to irresolvable disagreement among themselves: irresolvable, because they recognize no single, clear authority that can remove it. Another problem is that Roman Catholicism is itself unlikely to move any distance to meet them. It can move, and has done in the past, and the move is accepted by Roman Catholics because they do recognize an authority: if a change is authenticated by the Pope, it is almost universally accepted. But that happens seldom. The logic of this slow-changing authoritarianism is that when Roman Catholics, from the Pope down, speak of Christian reunion, they are much more likely to be thinking of the reabsorption of separated believers into a largely unchanged Roman Catholic Church than of a *rapprochement* in which each side would adopt certain beliefs from the other. Papal pronouncements on ecumenism no longer compel that interpretation, as they once did; but they leave room for it. In the Great Church thus created, Anglicans would find themselves asked to accept a degree of intellectual and moral discipline that they have not been used to.

Such a Church would have a head: a universal primate. This is common ground for ecumenists, and Roman Catholics could not be expected to accept it otherwise. Further, the inescapable candidate would be the reigning Pope: the venerability and prestige of the papacy, and the relative size of the Roman Catholic Communion, leave no other choice. On a certain view it would be untroublesome. Ecumenically minded leaders of the Reformed tradition in Britain were gratified by the courtesy which John Paul II showed them when he met them in 1982 at Canterbury; the Anglican-Roman-Catholic International Commission, a body that began considering these things in the late 1960s, believes that a universal primate would be guided by councils of bishops – many of whom, in the Great Church, would be from the Reformed tradition. But prediction does not have to rely on impressions and conjectures. There is a record to be studied. The declaration of papal infallibility in 1870, the dismissal of Anglican orders as null in 1896, the confirming of the ban on artificial birth control in 1968, the disciplining of insubordinate Roman Catholic theologians in the 1980s: these decisions, all of them taken in face of reasoned dissent from within Roman Catholicism, and none of them reversed on later advice, do nothing to suggest the kind of rule by consultation that Anglicans might find supportable. They are evidence of a plain tradition of autocracy, sustained for good or ill against all the political and social and intellectual pressures of the modern world. John Paul II represents the tradition accurately. It will not disappear when he does. To judge from reactions to his travels, it suits most Roman Catholics well enough. The sound of liberal protest can sometimes be heard, but matched by protest which finds the modern papacy not conservative enough. It is a tradition which would suit most Anglicans ill: so ill that they would simply set it on one side, and the whole ecumenical enterprise that had brought them to that point would have been for nothing.

The autocratic habit of mind is not papal only. It is episcopal and institutional. The Roman Catholic laity is not much consulted; and when it is, as by the Roman Catholic bishops of England and Wales at a National Pastoral Congress in Liverpool in 1980, its advice is not much regarded in Rome. That is wholly within the logic of a Church where authority flows down from its professional head; but it is not the culture in which Anglican laypeople now find themselves living. Journalists, similarly, are seldom taken to the bosom of the Vatican; and there is no reason why they should be, in a Church where attending to the questionings and remonstrances of laypeople is not the business in hand.

Simpler problems even than that beset the ecumenical endeavour. Evangelicalism is a vigorous and essential part of Anglicanism; and Evangelicals would have the greatest difficulty in accepting an Anglican reunion with Roman Catholicism, given their historic insistence on the authority not of the Church but of the Bible. A new Anglican-Roman-Catholic International Commission reported in 1987 on questions to do with salvation, where Roman Catholicism and Evangelicalism have traditionally differed, one finding it in the Church alone, the other in faith alone. The Commission has demonstrated to the satisfaction of its own members that if you phrase the differences carefully enough they will disappear. It may be so. There was an Anglican Evangelical voice on the Commission to vouch for the discovery. But if any arrangements for reunion were hung on it, Evangelical members of the General Synod of the Church of England, to look no further, would repudiate it massively.

And if, in a reciprocal change of heart without precedent in Christian history, Roman Catholics and Anglican Evangelicals were able to embrace; and if the whole of Anglicanism were then formally reunited with Roman Catholicism; and if the reunion extended, yet more remarkably, to all those scripturally based communions with whom Evangelicals feel varying degrees of sympathy – the Lutherans, the Baptists, the Methodists – Christian disunity would still be infinite. In the United Kingdom alone, union between Roman Catholicism and Presbyterianism (to say nothing of Free Presbyterianism in Northern Ireland) is inconceivable. The Presbyterian antipathy to personal as distinct from shared authority is too deep. Most determined of all in its zeal for private judgement and its rejection of all constituted authority outside the local group is the house-church movement. At an altogether different point on the ecclesiastical map, the Orthodox Churches (a significant presence in England) maintain the oldest of all separations from Rome. You could still argue that the mere fact of there being so many different Christianities is no reason not to try for a reduction in the number: fewer would mean better. But that would be to equate varieties of belief with phenomena like weeds. Perhaps the proper analogy is with flowers. And weeds or flowers, they continue to multiply. Historical precedents suggest that they always will.

It happens that the Roman Catholic Church is itself already engaged in ecumenical discussions with the Orthodox Churches, and sets great store by them. So is it engaged with the Lutherans. So is it with the Methodists. So is it with the Reformed (in the sense of Calvinist) Churches. So is Anglicanism, intermittently, with most of those Churches. The ecumenical dance goes on. It does no harm, as long as Churches can afford the airfares, unless raising unfulfillable expectations is harmful. It might do good, if it brought forward the general recognition that there are countless ways of worshipping the Christian God, and always will be, and every worshipper deserves respect and welcome from every other. That is the only necessary or attainable end.

10

Comprehensiveness

So the only Great Church possible is one within which a wide variety of Christian belief and practice is present and tolerated, and no attempt is made at homogenization. Such a Church exists already, in miniature. It is called Anglicanism.

Anglicanism has achieved those conditions because of the way it began. Under the Elizabethan settlement the Church of England was obliged to comprehend or enclose the two most sharply opposed forms of Christianity possible, one of them looking to authority, the other to private judgement; and it included many nuances within each one. As time went on it suffered departures at the edges. But a decently representative variety of belief remained, and remains. To get as good a start as Anglicanism did, a Great Church would need the Church of England's Tudor advantages reproduced on a world scale. It would need a powerful and well-led world Government; an almost universal sense that to be a citizen of the world was also to be a member of the world's Church; a common world language; and a liturgy in that language put together by a writer of genius. The conjuncture looks unlikely.

Anglicanism is therefore a rare growth. It nevertheless has the disadvantages of its advantages. Admitting many forms of Christian belief, it is in danger of appearing to maintain none. If people inside or outside Anglicanism are anxious to know what it stands for, they may not be able to discover.

Not all of that anxiety is respectable. It is a logical-positivist error to suppose that if a thing cannot be defined, it has no existence. (The example St Augustine gave was time: he knew perfectly well what it was until he was asked to say.) And certain kinds of believer want to know in detail what their sect asks them to believe in order that they may feel superior to everyone in or out of it who believes something different. Definition divides.

Definers are often forced back on metaphor, too; and metaphor can mislead. If you picture Anglicanism as a bag, or the shaded part of a Venn diagram, or a spectrum, or a continuum, it seems reasonable to ask where the outsides come; where the continuum runs from and to. But a different metaphor from any of those might carry the same quotient of truth without prompting the same question. Anglicanism might be represented as a sound, for example, sharp and clear at the point of origin, growing fainter as it spread circularly outwards, and yet with the point where it had finally faded to nothing almost impossible to identify, and different for different people.

Still, if the question is about what Anglicanism consists of at a minimum, and if metaphor is eschewed, as far as language allows, it ought to be possible to construct an answer.

Anglicans believe in God: benevolent, but not necessarily active, unless you count as divine activity the thoughts and actions of human beings when they do their best, prompted sometimes by their own prayer, to serve divine standards. Anglicans believe in Jesus, as having had a unique relation with God, and as therefore uniquely worth attending to as teacher and example. In particular, they believe in the religion of self-sacrificial love that Jesus both taught and demonstrated, however poorly they follow it out in practice. They believe in forgiveness in exchange for repentance. They believe that God will not abandon them after death. Most of them believe more than that; very few believe less.

To this can be added certain statements about the way Anglicanism is organized. It exists in many parts of the world. It is arranged in provinces, mostly corresponding to countries. Those provinces are autonomous. Anglicanism taken as a whole has no formal power over any of its provincial parts; but shared origin and friendship make them want to behave as far as possible in the same way as each other. They are all in communion with the see of Canterbury. Anglicanism is episcopal; the provinces are administered by bishops and archbishops. It is also synodical: bishops are joined in their work by elected synods that represent the clergy and the laity as well as the bishops themselves. In church, Anglicanism uses fixed liturgies, most of them distantly derived from medieval origins by way of the Book of Common Prayer. Much Anglican worship is in English still, but not all of it.

As for membership, you are an Anglican if you think you are. The terms are comprehensive. You are most incontrovertibly an Anglican if you have been confirmed by an Anglican bishop and go regularly to an Anglican church; and it may well be on those terms that you derive most benefit from your Anglicanism. But you are just as much an Anglican if you go regularly to an Anglican church, unconfirmed; or if you go only intermittently; or if the church you would go to if you ever went is Anglican; or if it is an Anglican church that you look to for the rites of passage, or that others look to on your behalf. There is no test of belief: there are no questions you must give the right answer to, from the heart, if you wish to come or stay inside. There are professions of belief made at baptisms and confirmations, and by the congregation at large at many other services; but they do not exclude the people who are not there to say them, or who say them with a certain mental reservation. That much can be said by way of definition.

It happens that mental reservation is made the easier, for Anglicans, because the main forms in which those professions are set out, the Apostles' and the Nicene Creeds, are very old. Even if their age were not directly known to the worshipper, it would be apparent from the loftiness and mysteriousness of their language. Those qualities are preserved even in modern versions like the ones in the Church of England's Alternative Service Book of 1980: 'by the power of the Holy Spirit he became incarnate of the Virgin Mary...' Suppose there is a phrase to which worshippers cannot entirely subscribe: 'he will come again to judge the living and the dead', or 'the resurrection of the body'. The language of the whole entitles any of them to say to themselves: 'Here is something my fellow Christians believed long ago: I respect it, but I need not accept it, because the lights they judged by were not the same as the lights we judge by.' If, on the other hand, a serious attempt had been made, in the Alternative Service Book or anywhere else, to rewrite the Creeds, removing the stumbling-blocks and putting what was left into plain language, the outcome would not merely give pointless offence to believers who took the Creeds from start to finish as statements of fact (and who might be right): it would deny to other believers the recourse of telling themselves that a point which troubled them was a requirement of ancient rather than modern belief.

That recourse is especially ready to hand when among the formularies of faith are included the Thirty-nine Articles. Article Four – originally put in, it seems, as a knock at sixteenth-century Anabaptism – states: 'Christ did truly arise again from death, and took again his body, with flesh, bones, and all things appertaining to the perfection of man's nature, wherewith he ascended into heaven, and there sitteth, until he return to judge all men at the last day.' A modern Anglican, knowing something of the irreversible effect that even a temporary heart stoppage can have on the human organism, or of the untraceability in space of anywhere where this bodily sitting might be going on, may judge that unbelievable. But this judgement is liberating, not embarrassing. If one part of the historic formulation of Anglican belief needs to be read or spoken with fingers crossed, as a product of its own time, then any part may be. A measure of scepticism is permissible. You may accept only parts of the package and still be counted an Anglican.

This comprehensiveness, this readiness to take in all kinds of believer, seems to me more than merely sensible. It is Christian. It is in line with some of the most readily self-authenticating things in the record of what Jesus said. 'Come unto me, all ye that labour and are heavy laden . . .'. It is a small paradigm of the mercy of God.

There are many Anglicans who are uneasy at this comprehensiveness; and that unease, too, is part of the Anglican tradition. Long after the Elizabethan settlement, the Church of England still resembled two teams in a tug-of-war: the Puritans and the Romanists were all hanging on to the same rope, but each side sought to pull the other clean across the middle line, so that Church of England belief should thereafter be of one kind only. Happily, they failed; and that failure, again, is part of the Anglican tradition. But the attempt continues; and presumably it will always continue, with the difference that the rope has become a loop and the tug-of-war many-cornered. Within each version of Anglicanism, there are believers who wish that the whole of Anglicanism were assimilated to their side. They seek new definitions of orthodoxy that encompass their own understanding of the truth and no other. They are abetted by those scholars who discuss authority, and attempt to devise or confirm new sources of it within Anglicanism, in order that modern Anglicans may receive fresh signals about which of the Thirty-nine Articles to believe and which not.

The attempt will not work, and it ought not to work. Since texts always need interpretation, authority cannot be vested in texts alone. The new authority would have to be human. It could not be merely episcopal, of the form of the Lambeth Conference or primates' meetings: the movement to listen also to the voices of other clergy and of laypeople, itself part of a general movement of ideas now hundreds of years old and impossible of reversal, has gone too far for that. Bishops cannot command obedience any longer, if they ever could. So the new authority would need to be synodical. But people would not take enough notice of that, either. They would be too well aware that a substantial proportion of the members of any synod in question had not read or thought much about the matter in hand.

A synod can determine issues of housekeeping: investment policy, levels of clergy fees, the setting up of new suffragan posts. It can respond to problems of the moment: a spurt in concern about freemasonry, or a Government plan for tax changes that will affect churches. In matters of that kind, someone has to make the required pronouncement, and a synod can weigh the arguments presented as well as any other body. More disputably, a synod can address many of those issues where a common practice is to be desired if things are to be done decently and in order: questions of liturgy and ministry. If a synod cannot impose uniformity in these things, it can at least lessen untidiness. Where a synod is for practical purposes useless is in matters of doctrine. It cannot command the necessary degree of assent. It might well be misled, by its numbers and its partial representativeness, into supposing that it could; and then it would be in danger of exercising the tyranny of the majority, which is as odious as any other kind of tyranny. A synod thus misled might forget that in a free association of reflective human beings, such as Anglicanism is, uniformity of belief is not to be had. It might set about declaring that certain people who thought themselves Anglicans were not in fact Anglicans. At that point, the genius of Anglicanism would be denied.

Definition divides. If Anglicanism were to go that way, it would steadily disintegrate. In one province or another, a new orthodoxy would be laid down. The losers, declared the heretics, would be obliged to leave. The winners would console themselves for their diminished national numbers and influence with the assurance that they were right. But then another province would feel impelled to respond to the first province's doctrinal assertions; and another, and another. These further statements would differ from the first statement, and from each other. In each country, adherents would again fall away; and internationally, Anglicanism would begin to lose its cohesion. Instead of being united by a number of accidentals, and divided by nothing visible, it would find itself in a state where the divisions looked deep and the unifiers unimportant. Whole provinces would leave the communion. The international self-confidence of the rest would droop. The process would accelerate until no two provinces were left standing beside one another. And no single view of Christian truth would have been advanced as a result.

I do not believe that this will happen. I believe that, instead, Anglicanism will remain a loose international conglomerate of Christians believing many different things. Its unity will be constantly strained: its members will be constantly tempted to disunity, but not above what most of them are able to bear. Anglicanism has the experience at containing differences, the tolerance of theological adventurousness, the confidence and prestige born of long existence, to carry this off. And truth, that elusive commodity made up of as many parts as matter itself, will be served as a result.

It is possible to be a little more precise than that, I think, about the form that Anglicanism will take in the future. In this book I have ventured several forecasts. Like much prophecy, they have an element of wishfulness in them; but I believe all of them are based in evidence and reason, and at least some of them will come true. For the convenience of readers (and in particular of fellow journalists, reading the book from the back if they read it at all), I set them out here again in summary. The time-scale is the next quarter-century or so.

The three main tendencies within Anglicanism, which can be called Evangelicalism, Catholicism and the middle way, each of them easily defensible both doctrinally and in terms of Christian lives lived within them, will all survive; and they will refuse synthesis. But Anglicanism will open its arms wider than to enclose just those three. Because of certain attributes of the parent Church of England, it is already unhostile to departures from doctrinal orthodoxy. Alongside doctrinal orthodoxy it will increasingly accommodate the idea of a God who does not act, and a unitarian God at that. It will be explicitly uncertain about an afterlife, and unassertive about the exclusive rightness of Christianity as against other faiths. Indeed, before long it will enter seriously on dialogue with other faiths.

In the Church of England, at any rate, old forms of worship will continue to lose ground to the new, and perhaps a little faster than is wise. Old churches, meanwhile, will go on being sold for secular uses like garden centres, or demolished, or incorporated into secular buildings; but perhaps more slowly than is wise.

The Anglican ministry will alter noticeably. Part-timers will multiply. Divorce in the priesthood will come to be regarded as a melancholy aspect of normality. Women priests will fairly rapidly become accepted throughout Anglicanism, and without much further strife or secession. Women bishops will come, too, and more troublesomely. The trouble could be limited if the first consecration, likely to be in the United States, were held off until at least the principle of women priests had been accepted in all other provinces. Although there may be schisms on the issue, they will be smaller than was at first thought likely, and will not prosper.

Bishops, male or female, will gain in importance as representatives of their clergy, even while they decline in formal authority over them. The number of bishops ought not to grow. They will be increasingly chosen as managers, not for scholarship or churchmanship or amiability. Already elected everywhere in Anglicanism except England, they will be chosen there too by a Crown Appointments Commission enlarged enough to have most of the properties of an indirect electorate. The chief effect will be to lessen the present influence of the Archbishop of Canterbury in the choice.

Establishment, though, also unique to England within Anglicanism, will never in so many words be abolished: it will pass imperceptibly away. Church of England provision of the rites of passage to all comers will be gradually curtailed. The present representation of the Church of England episcopate in the Lords will not last, because it is unfair to other Churches in the United Kingdom. It will be replaced by the only device that can accommodate them, a system of ecclesiastical life peerages. This reform will remove the last justification for such controls on Church of England business by Parliament as survive, and they will either be formally lifted or fall into disuse.

Some Anglican clerics and gatherings will continue to talk politics, and others will not: the tension between activism and quietism will persist, each of them having a decent case. On the whole it is easier for Anglicanism to be theologically than politically radical. Internationally, Anglicanism will need more identifiable leadership, of the representative kind, than it enjoys at present; and this cannot be supplied by the Archbishop of Canterbury, who will always be too busy and too English. It will have to come from a new-model Secretary General of the Anglican Consultative Council. The change will at any rate put paid to talk of an Archbishop of Canterbury from outside England. International mission, on the other hand, has little future, even if the historical flow from the developed to the developing world is reversed.

The ecumenical movement, too, has outlived its time of hope, though it has not been a failure: it has done something towards improving relations between Christians locally. All that is needed now is full mutual recognition between Churches

Achieving that is obstructed by the profitless search for something more. Churches will remain distinct. Anglicanism, therefore, will remain distinct. It will be recognizable by the way it is organized, by its forms of worship, and by its tolerance for varieties of belief.

That is the point, in the end. If Anglicanism can maintain its doctrinal comprehensiveness, as I believe it will, it has a precious future. It can do for Christendom what few other Churches can. Without turning away the orthodox believer, it can give Christian shelter to the unorthodox, to the doubter, to the half-believer, to the striver after fresh understanding. Remaining faithful to its own past, it can be a dispensary of Christian reassurance and a box for the pursuit of Christian truth. That is a reasonable service.

Bibliography

Books and pamphlets to which I am indebted, some of them mentioned in the text, are these:

Peter Calvocoressi, *A Time for Peace* (London: Hutchinson, 1987)

Owen Chadwick, *The Victorian Church* (London: A. & C. Black, 2 volumes: part I, 3rd edn 1971; part II, 2nd edn 1972)

The Church of England Year Book 1987 (London: Church House Publishing, 1987)

Colin Craston, ed., *Open to the Spirit: Anglicans and the Experience of Renewal* (London: Church House Publishing for the Anglican Consultative Council, 1987)

F. L. Cross and E. A. Livingstone, ed., *The Oxford Dictionary of the Christian Church* (Oxford: Oxford University Press, 2nd edn, 1974)

The Doctrine Commission of the Church of England, *We Believe in God* (London: Church House Publishing, 1987)

David L. Edwards, *Christian England* (London: Collins, 3 volumes, 1981, 1983 and 1984); *The Futures of Christianity* (London: Hodder and Stoughton, 1987); *Bishops and Beliefs* (Shepperton: Modern Churchmen's Union Pamphlet, 1987)

Alison Elliot and Duncan B. Forrester, ed., *The Scottish Churches and the Political Process Today* (Edinburgh: Centre for Theology and Public Issues, and Unit for the Study of Government in Scotland, University of Edinburgh, 1986)

Charles Gore, *The Philosophy of the Good Life* (London: John Murray, 1930)

John Habgood, *Church and Nation in a Secular Age* (London: Darton, Longman and Todd, 1983)

Augustus J. C. Hare, *Memorials of a Quiet Life* (London: Daldy, Isbister, 3 volumes, 1872)

Adrian Hastings, *A History of English Christianity 1920–1985* (London: Collins, 1986)

The House of Bishops of the General Synod of the Church of England, *The Ordination of Women to the Priesthood* (London: General Synod of the Church of England, 1987; GS 764)

Fanny Kingsley, ed., *Charles Kingsley: his Letters and Memories of his Life* (London: Macmillan, 2 volumes, 1877)

Hans Küng, *Christianity and the World Religions* (London: Collins, 1987)

Michael Marshall, *The Anglican Church Today and Tomorrow* (Oxford: Mowbray, 1984)

Robert Bernard Martin, *Tennyson: the Unquiet Heart* (Oxford: Oxford University Press, with Faber and Faber, 1980)

Hugh Montefiore, *So Near and Yet So Far* (London: SCM Press, 1986)

Peter Nott and Anthony Russell, *A Rural Strategy for the Church of England* (London: General Synod of the Church of England, 1986; GS Misc 247)

Oliver O'Donovan, *On the Thirty Nine Articles* (Exeter: Paternoster Press, 1986)

Francis Penhale, *Catholics in Crisis* (Oxford: Mowbray, 1986)

The Report of the Lambeth Conference 1978 (London: Church Information Office, 1978)

Michael Saward, *Evangelicals on the Move* (Oxford: Mowbray, 1987)

Stephen W. Sykes, ed., *Authority in the Anglican Communion* (Toronto: Anglican Book Centre, 1987)

P. K. Walker, *Rediscovering the Middle Way* (Oxford: Mowbray, 1988).

Maurice Wiles, *God's Action in the World* (London: SCM Press, 1986).

Index